TWO DOGS
AND A PARROT

TWO DOGS AND A PARROT

What Our Animal Friends
Can Teach Us About Life

JOAN CHITTISTER

For Maureen Tobin
without whom neither the animals' lives
—nor mine—
could have possibly been as happy.
With deep gratitude.

Published by
BlueBridge
An imprint of
United Tribes Media Inc.
Katonah, New York

www.bluebridgebooks.com

Originally published in hardcover in 2015 (ISBN 9781629190068).
First published in paperback in 2018 (ISBN 9781629190143).

Library of Congress Control Number: 2015945910

Cover design by Stefan Killen Design
Cover art: Friends, *Forbes, Elizabeth Adela Stanhope (1859–1912) /*
Private Collection / Bridgeman Images
Text design by Cynthia Dunne

Printed in the United States of America

10 9 8 7 6 5 4 3 2 1

CONTENTS

THE CAIQUE

INTRODUCTION

All my life I wanted a dog. After all, I was an only child. To a child without neighborhood friends, without sisters who could become eternal confidantes, without brothers as co-conspirators in life, a dog was the only obvious substitute for companionship. Or at least it was obvious to me. It was not at all obvious to my mother. Our house, my mother insisted, was not the kind of place where dogs belonged—a walk-up in a northern city given to lake-effect snowstorms. And furthermore, the landlord agreed with her.

But my mother could deal with the idea of my having a bird. On Good Friday, Billy, a blue parakeet, became the Easter gift of my life. Nothing has ever quite matched it since.

I couldn't take a bird for a walk, of course, as I had seen so many children my age do with their dogs. And we couldn't play ball together. But, on the other hand, I learned that having a bird meant having a companion where the interaction was more intense than it was with a dog. Dogs, at least to some extent, had a life of their own. Billy's whole life, on the other hand—every drop of water, every bite of food, every ounce of attention, every bit of play—depended on me. It was an amazingly warm and personal thought. It grew me up in ways I could never have expected.

"Joan," my mother said, "you taught that bird to eat out of your hand. Now you get home here and feed it." So, I quit the swimming lessons that were not half as important to me as Billy was, and did. Billy became my playmate, my ally, my first guide into the depth and meaning of the animal-human bond.

Billy came and filled my empty hours, learned to talk to me a little, flew to my finger when I called her off the curtain rods, woke me in the morning—and then, several years later, simply disappeared one day. And broke my heart.

No one knew how it had happened or where she'd gone. I only knew that, at the age of thirteen, I had lost something irreplaceable.

All over the world, everywhere, humans and animals form great bonds that give them both another kind of gift of life. Which is one of the reasons I'm writing this book. Nevertheless, I hesitate to begin it. A book of this nature brings with it a kind of intimacy and spiritual insight that seems to demand a special kind of privacy. After all, if you begin to talk about your pets as if such talk merits some kind of genuine attention, spiritual as well as psychological, what will people think?

So, this book has been in process for a long, long time. Years. In fact, I had to go through several levels of spiritual growth myself before I realized that it was, indeed, a book worth writing.

At first, I thought of it as nothing but the opportunity to tell a series of anecdotes about the animals I'd lived with in various stages of my life. After all, I had regaled groups for years with stories that smacked of depths far beyond either the usual tales of animal behavior or human appreciation of animal companions. Writing the stories down would simply provide the opportunity for a lot of people who like animals, who have lived with pets, to compare their own experiences to mine. Maybe to have a few laughs. Maybe to cry a tear or two.

Many of the stories, I knew, were funny. But some of them,

I also knew, were quite surprising for the level of spiritual insight they brought to my own understanding of the human-animal relationship.

Then, one day, in a public lecture I gave, I found myself beginning to explore the differences between the two creation stories in Genesis that have shaped the consciousness of the Judeo-Christian world for thousands of years. At that point, I suddenly realized that there is something quite spiritually profound in the question of what it means to be entrusted with nature, to live with a pet.

In the first creation story, Adam and Eve, first couple and prototypes of the human race that would come after them, are given dominion over what we call The Garden of Eden.

Who doesn't know the story? Who hasn't heard its conditions and its promises? Who doesn't take for granted the power conferred on humans there? Who doesn't recognize that, as part of the human condition, the story awards humankind dominance and precedence over all other living creatures?

The second creation story, however, far less commonly preached—in fact, commonly overlooked—challenges the reader in very different ways than the first. In this story, God the Creator brings the animals to Adam to be named—which, commentators commonly explained, is the proof that Adam had been given "power over them."

But, I could see, there are very serious problems with this interpretation.

Scholars tell us that this second creation story, which gives us the naming of the animals, is actually older than the so-called first creation story. It was, in other words, written earlier than the domination story. Only at a later period in biblical history

was this creation story about the naming of the animals reposi-
tioned. The effect of that kind of editing on the understanding
of the nature of creation and its implications for humans has
been momentous.

Clearly, the relationship between humans and animals had
once held a very prominent place, a very primary place, in the
human catalogue of spiritual lessons. The human-animal relationship had once held pride of place in the spiritual agendas
of human development. The repositioning of the naming story
not only made it secondary to the domination story. It also
made the dominance theme seem more basic, more fundamental, to human purpose.

God bringing the animals to Adam to be named was hardly
proof of "power." On the contrary. Naming is an act of relationship, not dominance. We name our children; we name our
friends; we name those with whom we develop an emotional
bond. But we do not name them in order to get power over
them. We name what is near and dear to us. We name the
animals we take into our families, the animals we commit ourselves to care for, the ones we take responsibility for, the ones
with whom we develop a personal relationship.

Naming gives our relationships character and recognition
and respect. Without doubt, then, the biblical story of naming
the animals has both personal and spiritual implications for the
way we deal with all the creatures of the earth.

The first creation story is the domination story. It defines the
process of creation from one level to another. It gives human
beings the right to use the rest of the planet for our own use.

The second creation story is the relationship story. By assert-
ing a particular bond between humans and animals, it inserts

us into the animal world and animals into ours—with everything that implies about interdependence.

With all of that in mind, I began to think differently about human-animal relationships. I began to realize what happens to human life and values when humans begin to separate themselves from the rest of life. Or worse yet, when humans begin to construct a hierarchy of life, with themselves at the untouchable top of it.

I began to comprehend more completely that life is about more than us. I began to understand that there is something necessarily spiritual about the human-animal alliance. There is something to explore there about the very nature of bondedness. There is something to be learned from relationships that demand more than words to make them real—and yet are clearly and certainly real, nevertheless.

More than that, there is also another level of reality that accounts for the writing of this book. The truth is that my own life demands it. I have never planted a flower. I have never staked a tomato plant. I have never watched anything grow or harvested it or had to wait for it to ripen in order to live.

Like most of the rest of the human race at this moment in history, I have been raised almost entirely in cities. And I have begun to see the effects of that on the human soul.

In the neighborhood where I live, we have children who have never dug up a potato, who have no idea where radishes and other vegetables come from, who are amazed to learn that peaches grow on trees. These are children who learn about food in cans and animals from picture books. And yet, pets are everywhere. So how to explain that?

The modern tendency to accept pets into our lives and our

homes is, I think, a subconscious human attempt to cling to nature in a world made of glass and steel that has divided us from it.

At least my own life is proof of that, and I recognize that as both a human and a spiritual lack. I also recognize that I am not the only one for whom this is true.

More than personal deprivation, social isolation, and emotional disconnectedness confront us as a species now. Crowded into high-rise apartment buildings, we are a century away from the smell of grass and the care for animal habitats. The effects of such physical and psychological distance from the natural world around us are sobering. It is the ability to destroy life without grief, to live life devoid of layers of consciousness, to develop technological relationships bare of affect.

And it shows. Our rain forests are being reduced to money. Our animals are being driven from their habitats to die on barren wastes while we wonder why they're disappearing. Our lakes and oceans are denuded from overfishing.

Unless we begin to align ourselves with nature, nature will be endangered and our own lives with it. Our own souls with it, in fact. We are here as part of creation, not as consumers of it. We are here to care for this planet, not to exploit it. We are here to find our proper place in it, to grow with it spiritually as well as physically.

But in order to do any of those things, we may need to rethink our theology as well as our role on the planet.

Seduced by a theology of superiority and domination, sure that the world and everything in it had been made for human consumption and human control, the narrative of human relationships with animals has a very mixed and sad history. Only the findings of science concerning the intelligence, feelings, and place of animals in the human enterprise, and the realization that we are all made of the same stuff, have begun once again to reverse the story of human-animal relationships and return it to an earlier cosmology.

We know now that if human beings disappeared tomorrow, the existence of birds, insects, water creatures, and land animals wouldn't be affected at all. If animals disappeared tomorrow, on the other hand, human beings could not possibly live without them—as long as bees are needed even to pollinate so many plants. As the top of the food chain, we would be the first to go. The interdependence of the species that has become so clear in our age has also shed new light on the concept of creation itself. The Creator of all, the scriptures tells us, saw all of creation as "good." It is our role to protect it, to guard it, to develop it, to sustain it—not to destroy it for our own purposes.

It is indeed time for us to begin to listen to the animals.

There are those who remind us now that the liberation of animals may well be the great liberation movement of this century.

But if that is the case, we must begin to think with the animals. We must begin to realize that they do not belong to us— they belong to God. They have lives of their own. And their lives affect ours. Whatever happens to the animals will eventually happen to the human animal.

This is a book about the role of animal companions in the development of our own spiritual lives. It is written for those who have pets and already understand that. It is also written for those who do not have pets and wonder why so many people do. It is a book about reestablishing the human-animal relationships Creation meant us to have. So, I am starting at the personal end of the subject—because my animal friends drew me out of myself and made me aware of another whole level of what it means to be alive. They gave me a much broader vision than it would have been if I had shaped it for myself out of nothing but work and time and things. In them, I have seen another face of God.

THE IRISH SETTER

DANNY COMES HOME

———

Acceptance

Danny was an unexpected birthday gift from a friend. The small convent, in the small town in which we were teaching at the time, was also "not the kind of place that dogs belonged," I suppose. But the difference was that this time, we all agreed to give the situation a try.

And that's where Danny came in.

Danny was a big red Irish setter. To those who know, the very name, Irish setter, rings of action and excitement and an unbounded, and unboundaried, love of life and of people. The problem was that I was not one of the people who knew that. Dogs were . . . dogs, I figured. Wrong. Dogs do not come in "one size fits all." Certainly not this one.

Danny was a total surprise to me, an absolute lexicon of lessons in life, the kinds of which I had never dreamed and was not expecting to learn. At least, not from a dog.

Which, of course, was the first spiritual lesson: Nothing and no one is exactly like anything else, no matter how much we may want them to be. The predictable is not what most pets bring us. They bring us life, yes. They bring us love, often. But predictability? Don't believe it.

Danny lived life on his own terms, and I learned to adjust.

Most startling of all, this wiggly, soft, and dewy-eyed puppy started his clawing, chewing search for independence and self-will early. It was the first night we had him, in fact.

I got the dog into the convent by promising the other sisters that Danny would stay in the empty garage that flanked our house on one of the main streets in the town. And I meant it. Students stayed after school that first day to build a doghouse for him in a dark corner of the garage, then lined it with covers, and secured a food and water bowl near its door.

We were hardly finished with the project when it was abandoned. "No dog can stay in that garage," the sisters told me. "No dog." Why? Because, they insisted, there were rats under the garage floor. Whether or not anyone had ever seen one, I'm not sure to this day. But since I didn't really want Danny there to begin with, I was quick to abandon the garage and bring the puppy through the front door squealing and squirming as we went. Now all I had to do was to rebuild the dog bed inside the house, at the foot of the basement stairs. Which, fortunately, were directly under my bedroom. From there I would be able to keep a watch on things. You know, control his puppyness, keep control, make sure that a dog did not disturb the good order of the convent. I wanted the relationship, yes, but on my terms, not his.

For the next three nights, I forced myself out of bed when the howling began. I groped for the roll of newspapers I had learned to keep on the floor beside me and stumbled down the stairs. The trick was to open the basement door and slap the newspaper roll against the wall—hard—till the new puppy was alarmed enough to stop the howling.

When he quieted down, I tiptoed back up the stairs, fell into bed exhausted, and waited for the howling to start again. Which it did. For one, two, and three straight days.

Finally, sleep-deprived and carrying a white flag, at three o'clock in the morning of the fourth night of this new relationship, I surrendered. I left the newspaper roll on the floor and went and got Danny instead. Patiently, but firmly, I put him on the throw rug beside my bed and went back to sleep. Until, with no small sense of alarm, I felt him squirm next to me. Clearly, this would take a little repetition for him to get the idea that he slept on the floor and I slept in the bed.

The second time he crawled in beside me, I took him off the bed and put him down on the floor again. And the third time, too. The night was going by quickly now. When it happened the fourth time, I figured out what to do. I attached the leash to his dog collar and put the other end of it under one of the legs of the dresser across the room. He could sleep on the rug at the foot of my bed for tonight. Tomorrow, he would go back to the basement where, more familiar with it now, I was sure he would finally sleep through the night. But for the rest of this night, at least, the problem had finally been solved.

Triumphant, I heaved a sigh of relief and fell deeply asleep.

It was when I felt something wet against my fingers that I knew I had a problem. I reached my hand above my head carefully and quietly and flipped on the bedroom light. There lay Danny the puppy tucked in tightly beside me, still leashed to the dresser he had managed to jockey all the way across the room. It was tilted now against the bottom of my bed. I unsnapped the leash, turned out the light for one last time, and let the dog go on sleeping where he was so I could sleep, too.

But I got it. There are some things in life that are simply not worth spending energy on. Danny knew what his priorities were; I had misunderstood mine. Danny was struggling to relate, to be accepted, to find a place in life that was worth reaching for, where he was safe and wanted and at home. I, on the other hand, was struggling to keep life within the boundaries I had independently defined for it years before Danny arrived to reshape it.

As Roger Caras put it, "If you don't own a dog, at least one, there is not necessarily anything wrong with you, but there may be something wrong with your life."

Until then, acceptance had never been high on my list of spiritual virtues. It was Danny who, that very first night, brought me face-to-face with the power of it.

———

Lao-tzu wrote, "Life is a series of natural and spontaneous changes. Don't resist them; that only creates sorrow. Let reality be reality. Let things flow naturally forward in whatever way they like."

It is at those times of acceptance that our souls come to peace with the world. Acceptance becomes the sacrament of the present moment, the point at which our struggle becomes useless and the unknown becomes the next step in life. If we learn to accept life as it is, as it must be—despite our best efforts to change it—we can keep on growing, even when we least want to.

All the great religions, too, teach acceptance of the vagaries of life and even signal this need for openness to life physically for all the world to see.

The Christian stands, for instance, hands uplifted to receive the grace of the moment—whatever it may be—with open hands. "Give us this day our daily bread," we pray. Give us, in other words, whatever it is that will nourish our souls the most, the best.

The Buddhist meditator sits cross-legged, stolid, trusting, inviting us to welcome life as it is—whatever else we might at that moment want it to be.

The rabbi stands, hands up, and pleads for the grace to welcome the unknown as friend, as sign of the presence of God.

The Muslim kneels, forehead bowed to the floor as sign of his submission to the Will of God, to what is happening.

It might take a while, but eventually we learn that accepting life as it is—learning to shape ourselves to it, rather than forever trying to wrench it to our own designs—is itself a virtue. It opens our souls to consider what parts of the present challenges of life must be changed—and must be accepted.

The kids in the neighborhood didn't accept the kid next door; he was a humpback and ran with flapping arms.

Rejection, I discovered, affects the way people view the world. Sometimes painfully. Always seriously.

The humpback kid kind of vanished into thin air. As a child, he was daily entertainment. He could be seen running up and down the street after other kids, trying to be included, wanting to be chosen—for anything. As the years went by and he got older, he stayed inside more and roamed the neighborhood less and less.

It was a study in the classic effects of rejection: Some of us become invisible, even to ourselves, feel worthless, cease to even try to be part of the crowd. Some of us became violent in our simmering reactions to exclusion, until one day we "snap" in public and people look puzzled and say, "I can't imagine what happened to him." The rest of us wilt and hide inside our houses, our workshops, ourselves, for the rest of our lives.

The lucky ones simply ignore the groups that won't take them and join other groups that will.

It's those groups, the ones who accept us, who teach us to accept the rest of life, as well. They enable us to trust that, in the end, we will find our way, be safe with someone, be cared for and grow. Everything will come out just fine—happy, life-giving, and lovingly secure.

Social acceptance, psychologists tell us, is a universal need bred into the human species by long childhoods and the lack of natural defenses.

They also tell us that social acceptance is absolutely fundamental to positive human development. Those who lack it, medical history reveals, live isolated and lonely lives, struggle with poor health, faltering immune systems, early death and depression.

DANNY AND THE SHOW RING

Self-Knowledge

Danny grew from a stringy-looking puppy with a long, bare tail into a sleek red silhouette of iconic proportions and noble beauty. I thought of all the great animal statues I'd seen—Man o' War, Lassie, Rin Tin Tin—and basked in the dignity of it all. There they were, champions all, and my dog, as well, a worthy carrier of his breed.

I washed him and groomed him, brushed his silken hair and trimmed his ears. His very stance, his gleaming red coat demanded it. But most of all, I wanted a well-trained dog, good in the neighborhood, stately guardian of the house, calm with callers, playful with children. Ah, yes, best of breed. The kind that returned the stick you threw and walked down Main

Street with you, nose next to the knee, never an inch of strain on the leash. I had seen far too many dogs walking their owners. I was an owner who wanted to walk a dog. In which case, my first step would have to be some kind of obedience school for dogs. The kind of school that trains service dogs and endurance dogs and military dogs and guard dogs. Dogs with character.

It didn't take long to find a group in town who met every week with the same ideals as my own and an experienced dog trainer who knew how to make it all happen. When I think back now, however, I realize that I had failed to notice something that was perhaps equally important. All the other dogs in the group, with the exception of two—the schnauzer and my Irish setter—were German shepherds. Had I processed that information consciously, I may have figured out sooner that there was a message in that.

Every day I went over to the riverside parking lot to put Danny through the paces: Sit, Heel, Down, Come, Stay. Sit, Heel, Down, Come, Stay.

It wasn't that Danny didn't get the drill. It was just that Danny didn't like the drill. He seemed glad enough to show me how quick he was at catching on. But he apparently didn't like the thought of having to repeat the process over and over again. The look on his face told it all: he frowned at me as if to say, "I did it—what else do you want?" In fact, I began to realize, the more often I required him to perform a command, the slower, the sloppier, the less snap there was to the routine. He was actually getting worse rather than better as the training time went by.

At the end of the course, dogs—OK, owners—got ribbons and statues and certificates that memorialized how trained they had become. Not mine. Danny got a little Grecian figurine marked "Most Lovable." And that was a clear message, too.

In fact, we did the obedience school caper a total of three times. But, as the Irish say, "There was not much between them." In every obedience training course, he did his trick once, bowed to the audience, and then opened his big red mouth, slid down on his haunches and yawned. This was not progress.

On the other hand, he did know the program. He understood the commands. He wasn't a slow learner. What he needed, I decided, was some genuine competition, a reason to perform, the feeling of achievement, the real thing. Not just one more night of walking in a training circle with dogs he didn't even know. I decided to take him to a dog show.

It was a gorgeous day. There were dogs and people everywhere. Families opened picnic baskets, sat on blankets and camp chairs around the ring, and watched dog after dog prance in and out of their formations.

When it was our turn, Danny "heeled" with the kind of brisk steps that got me thinking of animal statues again. He "came" on a trot. He "sat" on command. He "downed" to the ground with a heave. All of a sudden, I knew this was real, authentic, genuine. We were actually competing. Inching our way up the rungs of doggy greatness. Just a few more routines and we, too, would taste the glory of it all.

And then it came time to "stay."

To "stay," you are to put the dog in a "sit" command, turn your back to him, and walk away a good thirty paces or so before you turn and face your dog again. It is a three-minute exercise.

How long is a three-minute exercise for a dog? Well, put yourself in the dog's place.

Think of it this way: Someone has told you to stand on one foot for three minutes for no good reason at all. Or you are told to stretch and hold your arms out at shoulder height until you're allowed to put them down. Or someone wants you to sit in the snow or the sun or the rain until told to return to your seat, though whenever that might be, no one is entirely clear.

In this case, I gave the "stay" command with an air of authority, just the way the dog trainer had taught us. The trick was to plant the dog without hesitation, to make it clear to the dog that you knew what you were doing, and that you also knew what he was supposed to do. I walked away from him with a firm step and a confident air.

Danny looked at me and started to pant a bit and then to shift from haunch to haunch. I held my breath and pinned him with a stare. At the second minute, Danny began to look from side to side around the ring where babies squealed, "Doggy! Doggy!" all the while waving hot dogs in the air. At two and a half minutes, a big white standard poodle sashayed by, her nose up, tail wagging. Danny's ears went up, his nose went down, and he took off galloping across the ring and over the rope in hot pursuit. "Lady! Lady!" the judge yelled at me, "control your dog!"

Oh, sure.

It took an hour or so to find Danny, sitting at the edge of another family's blanket eating their Puppy Chow. There was a happy look on his face. Life had taken on an aura of joy again. He didn't look remorseful. He didn't cower when I showed up. He certainly didn't attempt to run away. He just rolled over on the ground and put his feet up in the air, paws collapsed, and the side of his mouth hanging lazily on the grass. Bliss.

And I? Well, Danny may not have learned what I wanted to teach him, but he certainly taught me a few things that day which are not to be forgotten: We are all what we are inside ourselves—and it is those things we need to develop. We are not here to become the pawns of someone else's ambitions.

We only went back to one more dog show after that, this time to conformation—the beauty pageant for dogs—rather than to the obedience trials. Danny was simply not made for obedience tricks. This time, though, Danny got a trophy for "Best in Show." And that was enough for us. Dog shows, especially obedience trials, were clearly for other kinds of dogs, not this one. So, as the Irish say, "We let them to it." We also let Danny go on to become his own unique self in ways that brought laughter to us all. I had wanted a dog with character, and I got a dog who was a character. And we were all the happier for it.

But I learned a lesson from his search for himself that has stood the test of time: Life is not about becoming someone else. Life is a matter of coming to be the best of what we are— and allowing ourselves to enjoy being it, at the same time.

———

The messages we get from the people around us can make or break what psychologists call our "self-esteem." The problem is that once those messages get skewed, it can take years to right them.

The child whose parents want a doctor in the family, for instance, has an immense burden to bear. To be loved by the mother, to be approved by the father, the child must do what she is not fit to do, or at least what she may not want to do. However capable, however constrained. So what is the right choice: family approval or personal satisfaction? And how do we know?

And yet the data are clear. To be healthy and happy we must all discover for ourselves who we really are. It is we who, in the end, must decide what it is that we ourselves are meant to become. To go through life feeling out of place, as interlopers on an alien planet or as refugees from our soul's real home, makes all of life a foreign land. We find ourselves where we do not belong. We chafe from the discomfort of it. And the wounds we suffer from suppressing one half of ourselves and pretending to be the other half sear our personalities and cloud our joys.

But self-esteem, the calm confidence that comes with being contented with who or what we are, is a great deal more than simply a state of mind. Self-esteem is the virtue of authenticity that comes with self-knowledge.

It is so easy to overshoot in life, to aim for stars that are not ours, to ignore our real talents and interests in order to become the flavor of the time. It is so easy to be seduced by the glamour of it all—of the exciting thoughts of what it must be to be astronauts or physicists or computer programmers or politicians or rock stars.

In an era of celebrity, the temptation is to forgo the joy of doing what we do best in order to do what the world around us applauds most. It is possible to chase the public dream of being an actress or politician or professional athlete, of course. But it is only our personal predilections, our genuine gifts, that can bring us to fullness of life. When we are really meant to be good farmers or brilliant pharmacists or great elementary teachers or kind counselors or skilled bricklayers, nothing else will do. To attempt to be other than what we are suited to be leaves the world a bit bereft and ourselves stranded in the desert of the self.

There is no amount of money, no degree of notoriety that can possibly compensate for the loss of the self. After all, how many boats can a person sail at one time, however much money we make doing what we do not really want to do in order to buy them? How large must a house be to contain happiness? How many corporate titles can possibly make getting up in the morning a happy thing to do?

The great question of life is, What will make me happy enough to be able to make everybody else around me happy, as well? The joy I bring to what I do will be exactly the measure of joy I have to give to those whose lives I touch because of it.

To reject our own talents in order to be measured by the seductions of a world leaves us unknown, even to ourselves. To be more bent on money than on fulfillment, on self-promotion rather than service, on acclaim rather than on interior depth, is a sin against creation.

We have all been given everything it takes to become the best of what we are. Life is a matter of discovering what that is and then, like birds in flight, refuse to be enticed off the mark by empty promises, by shallow goals. Life is the enterprise of learning how to become everything we are and all we want to do with it. Anything else is mere charade, a life only partially lived.

The lesson is that what we do best is what will make us most happy and most deeply effective. The life that is lived from the heart is the life that touches other hearts most. Then, the fullness of life will follow. Then we can learn to relax in it, arms open and a heart adrift in delight.

DANNY AND THE
AUTOMATIC DOOR

Enjoyment

Danny, the big red Irish setter, very quickly became the mascot without portfolio at the local high school in which we sisters taught. Which means that he didn't really do anything at all. He was simply there.

He didn't accompany the football team. He didn't jump with the cheerleaders. He didn't meet school buses in the morning. Because he couldn't be left home alone all day, he rode the convent van to the top of the hill every day and sat in the school office, waiting for someone to take him outside. There were candidates aplenty for the exercise.

He romped and caught balls thrown to him by errant gym classes. He accompanied the kids in detention while they picked up cans and paper cups on school property. The dog with the happy ending, he met reps, who came to negotiate orders of copy paper or art supplies, with a kind of hysterical joy. Danny liked new things, new people, new activities, new experiences. He did not much like the customary or the habitual or the ordinary. Which is why I was happy enough to let him roam and barely aware when he hadn't been around for awhile.

It was one of those days.

The school was full activity. Classes were getting ready for the annual open house extravaganza that brought parents to the school in droves. There were cardboard scenes and sets being painted in the gym and the cafeteria, each of them stood up against the banks of lockers that lined the halls. No, no one had seen Danny for awhile, but after all, he could be hiding behind any of those things. He would certainly appear soon, tail in high gear, ears up, eyes dancing.

By this time, he had become a fixture around the place. Everybody played with him. Everybody included him in class skits and daily walks around the outside of the school. He was the spoiled child of a very large family. It was the perfect place for him.

The high school sat at the top of a winding driveway, flanked on each side by woods that had been left to their own wild growth for years. The long driveway ran from the highway at the foot of the hill to encircle the school on a plateau that fronted another tree-covered hill behind it. In a setting like that, Danny could be anywhere and still be on school property.

So when the office phone rang, I was quite sure of the situation. A dog, the man on the phone told me, had been found circling the large, new grocery mart at the foot of the hill. In fact, the dog had become quite comfortable there. The better word, I think, would be "proprietary."

There was no problem with his being there, the manager was quick to assure us. Nonetheless, the staff thought that perhaps—well, maybe, in fact, surely—we were all very concerned to have what must be the school dog gone for so long.

Except, I explained, grateful as we were for their concern, it was not our dog. Our dog was right here. In the school. With us. No one had taken the dog out all day, I explained.

"Is your dog red?" the man asked.

"Yes, actually, he is," I answered.

"Then I think this is your dog, . . ." he trailed off. "He's been here a long time."

"Oh, no," I repeated. "He would never stay away a long time." This dog of ours was hopelessly addicted to the kids, I went on.

"Does your dog have a brown collar?" the man pressed.

"Yes," I said, "but . . ."

"Well, then, I really think that this is your dog."

"Look, I'm really sure this is not our dog," I said with a sigh, "but I will certainly have someone take another look."

The store manager was equally unperturbed. "Is your telephone number—which is why I'm calling—this one?" And he read off a number we'd had at the school for years. "Because it's right here on that collar."

I stopped short. Oh, good grief, it was true. Danny was at the grocery store bothering customers.

"Oh, I am so sorry," I gushed, embarrassed now and a bit irritated at the same time. "Just let him go. He'll come right up the hill, I'm sure," I said.

"Lady," the man countered, "We're not holding him. He simply won't quit it."

"Quit what?" I said, beginning to sense the doom, the inevitable. I began recounting to myself all the impossible things—the dead deer hip, the frozen suet can, the logs and boots and neighbor dogs—that we had become accustomed to watch Danny bring in the front door with him.

"He won't quit opening the new automatic door," the man said. "He has figured out that if he puts his paw on the rubber mat, the door swings open. It's been tap-tap, whoosh; tap-tap, whoosh; tap-tap, BANG! all morning long. Lady, this door is going to break if he doesn't quit this pretty soon!"

I imagined the cost of a new electric-eye door. I imagined what it would take to get anyone to give Danny a new home. I imagined what the headlines would look like in the small local newspaper that fed every home in the entire town.

"We'll be right down," I said, and sent two large boys and a good thick rope to drag him off the mat. This one was not going to be easy.

But inside myself I laughed all afternoon. I could see him now: his paw out, his nose down, his ruff up, his head snapping backward with every blow. Tap-tap, whoosh; tap-tap, whoosh; tap-tap, BANG!

The lesson was clear. We all need to enjoy what it means to be alive! We can't go through life with nothing to do but work or sit or laze or gaze vacuously at a gray, gray world. Uselessness is not a virtue. Nobody knew better than Danny that having fun is productive, that it confirms the possibility of new ways to live, that it teaches people to think differently. Most of all, Danny knew that having fun is not a waste of time; fun is what makes all of us lifelong learners of the joys of life. Life is an adventure that we must learn to make for ourselves. Enjoyment is important for us all. Life must have enough of its own electricity in it to make the most mundane of lives alive.

***

There is a myth about the spiritual world that does it a great disservice. The notion of this school of thought is that the spiritual life is an arena populated by the dour of soul, the dry of heart, and the neurotically well-disciplined. The purpose of life, they insist, is to beat out of life every ounce of fun, every moment of idleness, in order to demonstrate unequivocal commitment to spiritual growth.

In a spiritual world such as this, suffering becomes the real test of holiness. Endurance and repression of the self become its hallmarks.

But there is a serious flaw in this kind of thinking. The truth of the matter is that to repress the human spirit is to repress the work of the Holy Spirit itself. How can the creative spirit of the Creator continue to blow through the world if there are few souls open enough to detect it, let alone to receive it.

Enjoyment itself is a discipline. It means that we must become conscious of the goodness of life. It requires that we learn to enjoy just being alive. It insists that we give ourselves over to the randomness of the uncontainable. It snaps all the bonds that we have imposed upon the human soul and makes spirit more important than the system or the systematic.

Pleasure-seeking is what makes a society willing to explore possibilities. Only then can we come to know that what we fashion to meet today's stresses is more important than the rules we inherit from yesterday for dealing with them.

The more often we perfect the moves we've been given by someone else to produce, the less likely we will ever be to step out of the constraints of a history we have never been permitted to amend.

Pleasure-seeking enables a person to experiment outside the old norms. Without a fear of offending moral absolutes or corporate norms or social taboos, we can taste new ways of going about life. We can investigate the results of each. We can venture into new worlds of trial and error without the fear of losing either our lives or our reputations. It is the liberation of the present from the absolutes of a past long gone and enamored of them.

More than in any other age in history, our lives are molded by forces outside ourselves. We work to schedules created in other countries. We live in housing estates designed by developers who plot and plan according to standard measures: the acre, the plot, the size of a 9' x 12' rug. It is a standard-brand society that dulls the senses and numbs the mind. A world such as this needs mental refreshment that rigidly applied universal patterns do not encourage. Only the awareness that pleasure itself is a dimension of the healthy life can tear down the barriers and boundaries of the soul and allow what can be good to become real.

Pure pleasure, the right to function outside the margins of the normal, is the antidote to specialization. The robotization of the human community has become the way to define a market. We know what the young will buy because we have created their needs. We create a budget to predict an economy, whether the distribution of resources by it is equitable or not. We set standards and goals, we create categories and classes, to enable us to predict and propel the whole human race, lockstep style, from womb to tomb.

In such a world, the holiness of uselessness is at a premium. But the disparagement of personal appreciation for creative uselessness can take a great toll on a people. The stagnation of a society comes when we no longer take time to appreciate the smell of pumpkin pie or soak up the warmth of a fire or give way to the unbridled ecstasy of riding the rapids. We forget how to color outside the unyielding lines of our lives.

The sight of a society in quickstep attests to the obeisance we make to the great overarching rules of daily life. Only if we give ourselves over to the joy of life for its own sake can we challenge such a society from the bottom up, question its rigidities, refuse its norms.

Monotony is the enemy of new thought. Unless we find room for enjoyment in our lives, the more likely we are to become lobotomized by life. We stop thinking of other ways to live because we have already surrendered to the chains of it.

Sometimes just finding a way to entertain ourselves again outside all the work rules of the day, just breaking out of the daily, can change the very fabric and texture of our lives. We prove to ourselves that what *is* need not *be*, if we ourselves refuse to make it so. Louisa May Alcott wrote, "Have regular hours for work and play; make each day both useful and pleasant, and prove that you understand the worth of time by employing it well. Then youth will be delightful, old age will bring few regrets, and life will become a beautiful success."

Then we come to realize, in ways we have never realized

before, that enjoyment is of the essence of the virtue of hope. It is the proof that lies deep within us that things can be different, that we ourselves can make them different. Doing things differently is exactly what brings balance to lives burdened by the rigid confines of it all. It enables us to break through the perimeter of the standard. Then we find ourselves in the bright light of what it feels like to be new again, to be reenergized again, to be creators of our own destiny.

And, on the side, life itself takes on a more lively hue.

DANNY AT THE VET'S

Assertiveness

Danny's energy knew no bounds. He was a ball of perpetual motion, always alert, quivering with excitement over the most mundane parts of life: the postman on the porch, a dropped book upstairs, the crackle of aluminum foil on frozen fish. It was all one to Danny; everything in captivity was something to explore, a toy to play with, a treasure to carry away to some private Red Setter Shangri-la.

So when Danny got listless, slumped on the floor and did not respond to either ball or bone, there had to be something seriously wrong. He was about six months old by this time; it was our first trip to the vet and we were both nervous.

The office, on the other side of the river, was about a 20-minute drive from home. Danny clung to his blanket, head drooped over the edge of the backseat all the way over. But he moved willingly, it seemed, to the door of the office. Maybe this was not going to be as difficult an operation as I had feared.

When I finally got the office door open, however, Danny dug in, his nerves standing straight up on the back of his neck. There, in a large antiseptic waiting room, flat against three walls in rows of squarely placed thin metal chairs, sat what seemed to be the larger part of the town population. Each of them was holding in tow an animal that was every bit as nervous as Danny. There was a snarling Chihuahua; a growling German shepherd; several huge spitting cats; a variety of hunting dogs; and two large Doberman pinschers, every muscle taut, looking like they had been carved out of alabaster and straining to lunge.

Danny looked around the room, too, and froze on the doorstep. While every person in the room turned to watch the show, I had to drag him, face flat on the floor, over to the one remaining chair in the room.

The receptionist called each animal in order and by name—its own name, not the owner's—"Sweetie," "Bozo," "Baby Doll," "Thor," and finally, finally, finally, to my eternal relief: "Danny." By this time, the whole process had been at least as much an affront to my dignity as to his. I didn't know how he would feel about it, but I knew that I would definitely be happy to have the experience over and done with.

Inside the examination room, the doctor opened Danny's mouth to look down his throat, stretched his eyelids down to check his blood flow, raised his ears to take wax out of the ear canals, fingered his ribs, raised his tail and gave each testicle a quick but firm squeeze. Danny jumped a bit but gave not a sound. I could feel my sigh of relief go all the way to the soles of my feet.

"I think he's healthy enough, in general," the doctor said to me. "It's probably just a bit of a tummy bug. We'll give him a shot," he said as he moved toward the refrigerator to get out the vial of medicine. Danny watched with a wary eye but, all in all, we got out of the place with an acceptable degree of civility. Actually, I never thought about the incident again.

Until about six months later. Same scene—Danny listless and moping. Same examination, same diagnosis. Same treatment. The doctor came at Danny, raised his tail and made the shot short and sweet. This time Danny strained to get away, shook a bit and yipped, but we got out of there again, no worse for wear. I was beginning to feel like an expert at this thing.

By the third time we went, Danny was at least a year and a half old, a far more experienced dog. He walked into the waiting room head up and feet firm this time. He sat by the side of my chair and never moved till his name was called. I could feel him tighten a bit, of course, out of anticipation if nothing else. But nothing embarrassing. Nothing menacing.

This time the doctor went through the exam with a bit more deliberation. And Danny went through it with a bit more exasperation. The doctor had to pry his mouth open, and hold his head still as he stretched his eyelids, and put his arm around him to hold him still as he prodded his rib cage, and force his tail up to squeeze his testicles—one at a time. This time, Danny jumped backward and twisted away. The doctor, for his part, didn't seem to notice. "I think he's just prone to this intestinal infection," the doctor said. "However, the shot seems to be working for him so we might as well just give him the same thing again." I nodded and he moved to the refrigerator to fill the syringe.

But this time something in the regimen changed. The doctor opened the refrigerator door; Danny gave the doctor a long, hard look. He didn't snarl or snap. He didn't rear up or bare his teeth. He didn't pull on his pant leg or bite down on the doctor's hand. He just stood there and looked at him. And then, as soon as the vet reached out to raise his tail again, Danny took one step toward the doctor, raised his right leg as high as he could get it—and sprayed. With horror, I watched the yellow brew soak his nice white office coat, roll down the crease of the doctor's black worsted merino pants, cover his black leather shoes, and trickle across the linoleum-covered floor.

The doctor stood there, arm up in the air, syringe still filled with medicine, and watched what I was watching run down the floor between us. "Well," the doctor said and breathed a deep sigh. "I've had a lot of experience giving shots to dogs. I've just never had one tell me so clearly what he himself thought of the procedure."

When I think back now, it's clear to me that Danny's assertiveness in a situation like that was actually admirable. After all, the message couldn't have been more plain. A bit blunt, true, but at least not threatening enough to have the vet tell us that from now on we would need to find another doctor.

If truth were known, I don't like being poked and prodded, embarrassed and handled myself. And I'm not sure that I deal with those moments in life nearly as well as Danny did in that office, face-to-face with his nemesis. In fact, there is no amount of distress that any of us really ever get accustomed to. What we don't like, we don't like. What bothers us, we register. And then, like Danny, we also need to get it out of our system in ways that drain the venom but do not destroy the relationships.

We like to think that animals do not have the capacity for assertiveness that we do, that their responses to irritation are at least threatening, if not violent. But there it was, plain as the morning sun, in a veterinarian's office, in an animal hospital, right in front of my face. Faced with the needle one more time in life, Danny did not bark or growl at the doctor, snap or jump up at him, tear the pant cuff off his very expensive suit, or crash through his work table, spilling medicines and overturning boxes as he went.

No, instead, Danny simply turned his head to look at the doctor, stiffened his spine, raised one leg and made his point. Clearly. Plainly. And without rancor.

If only I could be sure to do so well.

―――――

Before 1945, most business was local, built on long-term, face-to-face contacts and a reputation for integrity. Postwar American business, on the other hand, found itself in a televised world, having to learn how to be nice to people they would never meet but must surely influence.

Suddenly, public relations and corporate honesty became new kinds of public virtue.

The virtue of honesty became the ability to own my feelings—without being willing to destroy the other because of them.

Human relationships had suddenly become a public service as well as a virtue, a virtue as well as a skill. They were, in fact, fundamental dimensions of real life, the very foundation of commercial life as well as the essence of the good life.

But could you really trust a businessperson anymore? Would

they tell you the truth—or would they tell you only what they wanted you to hear?

Real truth-telling, real assertiveness, admits the hidden dark spots of life and sets out to shine a light there, rather than simply masking irritation with polite dishonesty. Real assertiveness is the virtue that makes the difference between social charade and human honesty. It teaches us that what is always true is not always right to say, unless it can be said rightly. Meaning, without acrimony—as well as without subterfuge. Plainly.

The notion of truth ordaining the right to revenge becomes bogus in the light of spiritual maturity. The claim that retaliation is a justifiable response in order to settle a still sore score against my dignity dies aborning in the spirituality of assertiveness. The claim that past wounds are any warrant for eternal enmity loses merit immediately.

Instead, the world begins to turn on notions that are meant to soften life at its hardest moments and bring love where the same small seed of hurt is most likely to foment hate.

Assertiveness enables us to respond to indignity, to affront, to assault, and to abuses of power without becoming what we hate. It brings us to the awareness that we have both the right and the responsibility—in the interests of honesty and human dignity—to state our cause, to make our cries of wrong clear, to assert our rights, and, at the same time, to present our case in hopes of receiving an equally civil response.

Self-discipline grounds the virtuous life in reality rather than self-satisfaction. An instant gratification mentality waits for nothing and no one to satisfy my whims, my fancies, my expectations. But self-discipline honors the right of the other to have needs and obligations different from my own, even while insisting on the right to claim my own.

Walter Mischel's classic Stanford Marshmallow Study, which began in the 1960s, gave preschoolers the right to choose one of two options. They could decide to eat the one small reward that had been put in front of them immediately. Or they could wait until the experimenter returned to the room to give them a second small reward for being willing to wait. Those who decided to forgo the immediate reward were found, in major studies decades later, to have been more likely to complete their educations, stay married, have more career success, and be less likely to have struggled with addictions.

The ability to forgo emotional satisfaction in the moment led, it seems, to more and greater rewards in the future.

How all of this works, we may not know. But we do know that there is a difference in life patterns between those who deny themselves instantaneous gratification, and those who do not. We also know a few other things, as well.

We know that assertiveness—nonviolent as it may be—is not passivity, it is grace under pressure. It is not weakness presented as a substitute for strength. It is the opportunity to bring our own emotional responses to heel while we make our intellectual needs and reactions clear. It bolsters character. It enables us to bring new insight—in peaceful ways—to errors too long tolerated in the name of peace.

DANNY AT THE SHORE

Purpose

The thing about Danny was that once he focused on something, there was no getting him away from it. Sometimes it worked in your favor—sometimes it didn't.

There was the day, for instance, when Danny laid down his life to rescue me from a problem I didn't have. And that protectiveness itself became the problem.

It was one of those August meetings on the shore, held long after the color had left the summer rose. The agenda shifted from dull to intense as the sun rose higher in the sky and the temperature went from dry to hot to overheated to sticky. We were in an old house that had been built more for ocean breezes than for air-conditioning. It didn't take a psychology degree to know that, unless some regular recess, some privacy, some kind of mental relaxation were built into the schedule, this meeting was doomed.

The hardworking, tired women sitting in this room had already borne the summer heat and the inconveniences of travel just to get here. To maintain any kind of concentration, let alone energy and interest in the agenda from one end to another, things had to loosen up, and soon. I was always fond of telling process designers that "the break you do not give people, they will eventually take—whether you give it to them or not. And exactly when you most want their attention." It had always been my experience that young, ambitious, hard-driving directors always learned this secret of professional productivity the hard way. In the end, the mind is its own manager.

I was hoping to avoid that pitfall this time. After all, this commission only met once a year.

We were the happy guests of a group who had a guesthouse on the boardwalk in Atlantic City, one of the great playgrounds of the United States. What could be better?

We decided that business sessions would begin immediately after prayer and breakfast every day. The sunbeaten early afternoons, however, we reserved for quiet time—time to sit on the beach, good time in the ocean for those who liked a quick swim. If nothing else, time for a brisk walk on the boardwalk, drawn by the smells of cotton candy and candied apples or the lure of funky souvenirs. For some it was as simple as riding down the boardwalk in a colorful old open-air electric cart that had been plying the walkway for decades.

Almost anything is possible on the boardwalk. Except for one thing.

The signs were clear and the signs were everywhere: under

no conditions were dogs allowed on the beach. Crabs, maybe; cats, perhaps; I even saw a man with a monkey on his shoulder. But dogs, never! What had seemed like the perfect holiday for an Irish setter, for a water dog, went to dust the minute we parked the car.

When we left the house to go to the beach that first afternoon, Danny lay stretched out from one side of the porch screen door to the other. He was clearly laboring for breath, sucking hard to catch a hope of a breeze. But not one ruffle of air crossed his chest, not one clump of his heavy red hair fluttered. I could hear the panting all the way to the kitchen. I took the door farthest away from the beach so I wouldn't have to suffer his disapproving look, so he couldn't see the big beach towel over my arm.

Out in the water, we paddled around together telling stories, moving further and further out into the deep. The object was to keep our shoulders protected from the sun by keeping them underwater while we basked in the cold ocean on a steaming day. It was a delicious moment. You could see the women come alert one at a time. By the time we went back to the meeting, the worst of the sun would have gone and we would be able to think again, tension gone, spirits high. Mission accomplished.

The recall of the event from the person who stayed on the porch is a slightly different one, however. The woman who had stayed behind to type up the notes from the morning session had a feeling, she told us later, that something was about to happen. Danny, she said, figured the whole thing out the minute the house got quiet.

First, he paced back and forth between her desk and the high, wide screened-in windows, stretching up to see over the ledge of them. One of the women saw him at the screen and waved and called back to him, "Hi, Danny; Hi, Danny; Hi, Danny . . ." It was right out of a scene from *Lassie Come Home*. Except that the sight of all of us, far from shore and up to our necks in water, set off something in Danny beyond mere interest, beyond anxiety. Beyond anything even close to his excitement during playtime on the school hill. This time Danny was leaping straight up the window screens, looking like he'd been ejected from a jack-in-the-box.

The frenzy grew. More overwrought than ever now, Danny began to run around in circles. Then the running got faster and the howling started. It was too late. Before she could distract him or I could stop the squealing women from waving at him in the water, it was over. Danny reared up against the back wall of the farthest room in the house. He gave a throaty rolling growl, lunged through two rooms, leapt over the table on the porch, and sailed straight through the screened-in window.

The scene after that roiled the whole beach. He fell a good ten feet to the patio tiles beneath him, hesitated not a second and got faster and faster as he headed under the boardwalk. Kicking up a trail of sand on his way to the water, he swam for dear life, eyes wild, ears flapping. And straight at me. By now everyone on the beach was waving straight at me and shouting, "You have to get your dog out of here. You have to get your dog."

I turned my back and put everything I had into doing one of those great impressions of an "I-know-not-the-dog" routines, but it was no use. By this time, he was only feet away from me. I felt him grab the strap of my bathing suit and begin the tug toward the beach.

It took the rest of the afternoon to find a large enough piece of new screening and get the broken frame repaired. But there are some things in life that we can only learn when they happen to us. Yes, I had been rescued from a problem I did not have. Yes, in fact, the rescue itself was the problem. Ah, well, so what? I knew now as I had never known: Danny and I were a team. No amount of propriety could ever have substituted for that. It was one of those "until death do us part" moments in life, the kind for which you're willing to take any amount of public ridicule.

I watched a mild, playful rogue of a dog become a fierce and mighty savior in front of my very eyes. If a dog can do that, I thought, then surely I can devote myself to something worthwhile at least as much.

In the deepest part of each of us there are always two things: the desire to become everything we can be, and the need to find out exactly what that is. At the convergence of these two roads—at the point where faith in self becomes faith in something greater than ourselves—lies the meaning of life.

This road to self-development and self-definition is not an easy road, nor is it commonly a direct one. We do a lot of seeking, a lot of changing, a lot of becoming before we finally get to the point of finding ourselves, of becoming ourselves. It is a life of try and fail, of seek and not find, of start and stop. Who hasn't felt a sense of incompleteness, of unfinishedness in life, only to discover that being finished is not always what life is meant to be about. Most of life is simply about finding the more of us, rather than finding the whole of us. It is about summoning up within us what is needed in each particular moment of life—rather than resting on those parts of us long successful but long static, as well. Always allowing the rest of us to emerge, to become our best possible self, may well be the truest definition of life we will ever enjoy.

To know early on what it is that burns inside of us to such a degree that we can follow the light of it to the very end is one of the great graces of life. The dim, quiet flicker of purpose within us is the light that never goes out. It is the answer to the age-old adult question that every generation imposes on the generation after it; it is the need to discover what we want to be when we grow up.

The truth is that the passion that drives us in later years is already within us. It cannot be given to us by anyone else—the father whose ambition for us is security, the mother whose dream for us is fame. It can only be glimpsed in the fleeting pieces of the self that shine through us at the most private, most unplotted, most spontaneous moments of our lives. Then the answer to what we're meant to do in life comes in Delphic ways, in short bursts of insight meant to be interpreted with the future in mind.

The paradox of personal purpose lies in the fact that most of us can trace the seed of it in us back to the earliest moments of our lives. It begins to stir within us in inarticulate, unshaped, amorphous, and mystical ways. We look back years later and discover that the answer to what we were, to what we wanted to be, to what we really loved, to what we wanted to spend life on, had simmered in us for years.

Children who grow up to be engineers remember that they always loved to play with construction toys. Storytellers in film and advertising and literature and theater remember organizing plays for the other children in the neighborhood. Healers remember years of bringing home injured animals to save. Artists and architects find, years later, the pictures they drew on the underside of the dining room table or on the walls of their bedroom closets. Business people who wind up in corporation sales programs or investment banks later tell tales of selling the Sunday newspaper back for pennies to the grandfather who was reading it at the time.

The point is that there is a core in us all out of which come the strongest, clearest, most basic drives we'll ever know. Under stress, driven by need or despair or fear, it is this great drive that rises within us to prod us on, to give us hope. This great primitive direction of the heart makes us strong in times of greatest weakness, deepest need. It becomes the fire that burns away all the obstacles that lie between us and our heart's desire.

Those for whom this fire of life has never been sparked, those in whom this fire has been damped, risk dying without ever having fully lived. Those in whom there is no memory of purpose or great potential or sure destiny or untasted identity live life on a plain of dull, dry dust. Then life lacks taste. Life grows dull.

But for those who know within themselves this driving, leaping sense of purpose, life is constant becoming. For some, this great burst of certainty about who I am and what I was made to do in life is a clear and ringing call. Then there is no mistaking the moment of fulfillment when it comes. Then we speak our truth to power. Then we expend ourselves without measure and without limit for the sake of a purpose greater than our own aggrandizement, more meaningful to me than even my own interests.

It is this that drives simple people—the Franz Jägerstätters or Dorothy Days or Martin Luther King, Jrs. of this world— to become spokespeople for those even more vulnerable than themselves. This is the kind of personal insight and holy faith that carries astronauts into space and visionaries into politics and holy people into martyrdom. It is this sense of purpose and commitment that makes us who we are and confirms why we have come to this earth—and why it is a better place because we are here.

There is simply something in life that all of us are meant to do. And someday the moment will come when, if we are true to ourselves, we will do it.

DANNY AND WORK

Balance

Danny was one of those dogs who loved everybody—and a few people more than others. Which means that he was a basically pleasant member of the family who could—and would, under certain circumstances—feel jealous, rejected, overlooked, put upon, and proprietary. Depending, of course, on the moment, the persons, the situation. He was, in other words, just like us—only more so. All of those emotions are apparent in us, too, but we know how to mask them. He didn't.

The problem was that Danny did not get to talk to anyone about it. Or "work it out," as they say. Or apologize. You had to respond to it or he would pout. Then, it was up to you to figure out what had gone sour in the relationship and do something to change it. Which, come to think about it, is pretty good advice for all things human, as well.

For instance, guests were the high point of Danny's life. He would bound to the window to watch them come up the porch steps and then race around the corner of the hall to meet them at the door, as well. Obedience school hadn't all been for nothing, at least. He didn't jump or bark at people. He didn't push or shove. And he didn't, heaven forbid, bite guests at a monastery door. He just stood nervously in our midst, head back, panting and wagging his tail to the point of distraction, shivering with excitement. Waiting for the moment of his own grand entry into the conversation.

With one exception. If any visitors made a move, arms open, toward me, Danny—almost six feet tall on his hind legs—moved like a gazelle between us. With one swing of that strong but innocent-looking tail, he could bump an unwary stranger off balance long enough to wrap his long paws around my neck himself. Any experienced psychologist would not have been fooled. Yes, there was a hint of a smile on Danny's face.

At the same time, friendly as he was to strangers, he was more than willing to see less of them if they interrupted his own need to be noticed and appreciated.

There was the time, for instance, that one of the chairwomen of the group came to work on the final draft of a national document. Danny had already sat under the large dining room table for two long days, never making a sound. Just waiting. You could read it in his eyes: any minute now, surely, we would take a walk, go to the park, play ball in the living room. By the third day of work, with barely a pat on the head, let alone a walk, it was clear this would not be tolerated much longer. The rolling and sighing and pawing had already started.

By mid-afternoon, patience was no longer an option. When

the chairwoman finally got up to get another pen, Danny got up as well. He stepped up onto her chair and then moved from there to the tabletop. One paw at a time, he ceremoniously raked every piece of paper on the table—hundreds of them, all unnumbered—off onto the floor. I got the message. Yes, I had failed him badly that week; but he would just have to get used to it.

Famous last words.

For instance, at another time, in the presence of another professional visitor with major organizational problems to resolve, the conversation went very, very late.

At long last, only the two of us were left in the room with the data in hand and only this one long night left in which to evaluate it. We were in a room whose doors led to two other, connected rooms. Our conversation was intense and concentrated but I found my attention slipping, nevertheless. I was distracted by something, but I could not for the life of me figure out what it was.

At last I became aware of Danny brushing between us, a kind of gambol to his step. But the visitor was deep in conversation and Danny was being quiet, so though it was well beyond work time, I paid no attention at all to the clock.

Then I realized that Danny was making the circle of the three rooms. He would leave our room through one door, come back in through the other door, and trace the circle all over again.

And I noticed what I had not seen before. His legs were getting higher as he went. Like a horse doing dressage or a parade troop of cavalry prancing down a boulevard, he cavorted from room to room. There had to be something going on. Dogs don't run like that.

Finally, as he went by for the fifth or sixth time, his eyes flashing frantically, I saw it: There, in front of Danny's face, was a small round plate hanging, it seemed in midair. Impossible! I thought. And then it dawned: the plate he was trying with all his might to shake off was the butter plate the cook had left out to soften for the breakfast toast. All four of his great canines were embedded in frozen butter so solid, no amount of prancing could possibly have dislodged it for hours.

Bored by our incessant talking, Danny had taken it upon himself—denied any kind of human attention—to find another way to amuse himself. He simply walked by the kitchen countertop, tipped his head to the side, and came up with the pound of butter that was there for the taking. And the plate it came on, as well.

The lesson was plain. Everybody needs attention. Work, no matter how good, how holy it is, is simply not enough to fuel the human being to fullness. Most of all, it is nowhere near as important as human relationships. There is time enough for everything in life. It is simply a matter of allowing ourselves, of training ourselves, to take it.

Danny did everything he could to help me understand these things.

In a culture that bases its success on productivity, everything else in life becomes a by-product, an also-ran, an aside. The important thing in a world like this is work. Life, real life, gets squeezed in between work hours, and time itself becomes an obsession. So many minutes for this; so many hours for that. In the event the universe does not yield to our scheduling demands, we engage even more people to work even harder to try to make it happen. Or we beat the job down to size till it becomes half its quality, rather than take the time to do it properly. Productivity trumps quality. Quality gives way to mediocrity. Beauty and art, skill and expertise, surrender to mass production.

It is a world that begins and ends with the creation of things instead of the development of friends and family. And so we wind up with the glorification of the products rather than with the humanity of the producer.

A system like that touches every dimension of our lives, throws everything off balance.

When we overschedule our days, the success of them is counted by the number of things we get "done." Failure becomes defined not so much by shoddy production, but by our inability to keep up. Life becomes a marathon of checkmarks based on meeting all the appointments, producing all the reports, making all the trips, resolving all the issues, reading all the emails. As if they wouldn't still be there tomorrow, no matter how much time we spend on them today.

The very thought of living life well between the end of work one day and the beginning of work the next is a thing of the past. The notion that we might live life after work hours in ways that enhance its quality has taken on an aura of absurdity in this age. It marks us as people of whimsy, carriers of a touch of madness which, if not cured, could easily infect the entire society.

It's not that work is not important. But work is not all of life. And when it is, the rest of life suffers to the point that the work itself will, in the end, be seriously affected.

Few of us divide the day into distinct parts anymore. Nor do we even insist on dividing the whole of life into phases we promise to consider consciously. Americans, sociologists tell us, don't even take regular vacations anymore. They take "long weekends."

And yet, life is lived best when all of its component parts are attended to. The right balance. Which means living a life that makes defined time for family and friends and recreation and food and health and self-development and, oh yes, work. One thing we know for sure, however: if any of these parts is not attended to properly, they have a way of intruding into life just when we are least able to deal with them. One of the children gets sick and leaves us with a serious treatment regime and high bills, for instance. But there is no one there. No one to take care of the situation for us as life goes on already over-loaded, already stressful enough just as it is. Too much of that kind of thing and the nervous system snaps; our relationships sag; our health declines. And we can't imagine why. Tomorrow becomes more burden than joy because it is always just more of the same, too much more of the same. The quality of our work disintegrates, someone else is promoted, and we are left at the bottom of everything, trying to start all over. Then, however much our need for control, we realize that we have come to the point where we are no longer in charge of life. Instead, life, shattered and fatigued, has taken charge of us.

The world is willing to allow us to work our hearts out if we want to, but not without paying due service to the rest of our lives as partners, friends, and family together. A romp in the yard with the children after lunch, for instance, is always in order. A good supper taken at ease with a few laughs as entrée to a pleasant and restful night needs to be de rigueur. Family and friends and food are of the essence of life. Not papers and work hours and frowns that go far into the night without even so much as a smile and a conversation for anyone else.

When work, rather than play or rest, spiritual reflection or pauses for praise, is wanting, it is time to take drastic measures to right the planet on its axis. It is time for the outrageous and the unexpected. It is time to toss the apple barrel and start again.

DANNY
THE COUNSELOR

Empathy

The woman had been coming to the monastery to see me for several months now. She was a fragile but valiant personality. Nothing much ever changed in her life, but she went on functioning regardless. The problem, of course, was that nothing ever improved much, either. Perhaps the best way to say it is simply, "she soldiered on." She never completely collapsed emotionally, but neither did she ever manage to break out of the emotional chains that held her rigid and brittle in the winds of life.

I had been listening to her carefully, session after session, asking what I thought were probative questions, hoping for the breakthrough that would end the agonies. I went from one side of a question to the other, seeking the insights that lead people to begin to look at their lives differently. Every opening seemed to be a dead end. "Few people really want to live their lives differently," an old spiritual director had told me somewhere along the line. "They want comfort; they don't want change." In this case I had begun to give that possibility serious consideration.

In her case, she went through the routines of life from week to week and then came back to talk listlessly about the listlessness in her life.

I looked in vain for glimmers of enlightenment in her eyes, but there was only dullness there. I watched for some lift in her shoulders, hoping that some new life had come into her from somewhere that we could at least begin to build on. But so far, none of that had happened. Not even in the most minute of ways. She was disappointed in the process, I'm sure. I know that I was. I had even begun to think about passing her on to some other counselor in the hope of finding a better fit for her. Maybe someone with a more acute, even more personal, understanding of her struggles could be more help to her than I was being.

Somehow there had to be a way to ignite some feeling in her and then, hopefully, some desire to go on feeling good. She needed to get back in charge of her own feelings. She needed to feel them spark and grow again.

I watched her bend over on the seat, tears in her voice but not on her face. Never on her face. Her posture said it all: she was smothering under the weight of her own life and too emotionally exhausted to do anything but talk about it. Just to sense the tears in her voice, however, gave me hope. Everything up to this time had never been anything but recitation. Maybe now we could really begin to touch the feelings that went with them. My own heart stirred at the thought. Finally.

Then, all of a sudden, I heard it. Just a small tingle of a sound, but definitely a sound. I froze, instantly alert, deeply apprehensive. She was sitting on a light two-seater sofa along one wall and went right on talking.

I, on the other hand, was sitting on a chair along the adjoining wall. I could see both her and the large desk across the room. And then I recognized the sound.

Under that desk across the room, the big red setter, much older now, lay sleeping. I also knew that this was a woman who did not really like dogs. At least she had never shown any interest in him. Just to be safe, I had always remembered to take him out of the room before she arrived. But not today. I took in breath and said one of those great private prayers that are more hope than piety. As in, "Dear God, do not let that dog come out now! He will ruin everything!"

Nevertheless, prayer or no prayer, I already knew that it was all too late. The jig was up. All ruined before it had ever even begun. I could hear Danny under the desk, lumbering from one side of drawers to the other, stretching his legs, rising to his full height, and pushing back on the desk chair to extricate himself. His long, graying head appeared around the corner of the desk. Inside myself I refused the inevitable and tried to scowl him into place. Not on your life!

The dog looked at the woman and then at me. At her—and back at me again. The frown accented his white eyebrows as he shook the sleep out of himself and began walking gingerly across the room, his old legs creaking as he came.

My hope was to take him by the collar when he got to me and then push him quietly into the anteroom behind us. But no, instead, Danny changed course and went straight to the woman frozen into silence on the sofa.

He put his great mottled head down squarely on her lap, his head tilted back, his eyes melting into hers, one soft, broad paw raised on her knee.

Then, without even so much as a glance at me, she took his big bony head in her hands and began to talk to him. "You understand, don't you, Danny? You know what it is to have no one who understands you? You understand . . ." and the tears let loose in one great gasp. She bent over him, holding him ever more tightly, and cried and cried and cried.

I didn't move. I just watched as he raised his head even higher, pressed it flat up her breast, and nuzzled into her neck. Then, when the sobs had quieted for a while, he threw a look back at me. An accusatory look. As in, "Did you do this to her?!" and lay down at her feet.

She was ready now. It had happened. Rubbing his head as she spoke, all the great hurts of the past came out and the way to the future opened with a rush.

I learned a lot that day about empathy—when sympathy is meaningless and feeling means more than talk. Danny did not see the tears and pass them by. Danny felt those tears and stayed in them himself till they stopped.

———

We have all learned that virtue has something to do with doing something. Doing good things for people who cannot do them for themselves.

We hold clothing drives for the homeless and know without doubt that we have done good.

We serve soup to the hungry and realize the holiness of it.

We risk our own lives to bring water to refugees in the desert.

We build houses for the homeless, and care for prisoners, and bury the dead.

We do all the corporal works of mercy with joy, maybe because the effects of them are so obvious.

But, at the same time, it's difficult, in a culture that prizes the pragmatic more than it does the spiritual dimensions of life, to imagine that presence itself is a balm. The act of simply being present to pain may be at least as powerful a gift as anything we can make and leave on a doorstep. To have been broken is to know that the genius of understanding is as impactful as action can ever be where feelings are foreign or pain is dismissed.

We forget that every problem in life may not be able to be resolved—here and now and always and forever. And yet, at the same time, it is true that understanding can mean more to the person trapped in torment than a donation does.

Support, not bogus solutions or the temporary suspension of reality, is what makes life worth living, actually possible, certainly less lonely, surely less desolate. It's support, the surety that there will be someone who stands by when everything else in life has failed, that saves us from despair. It's someone who understands the burden I'm carrying—even if there is nothing they can do to help me lift it—that reduces the weight of the load. It's knowing that someone, anyone, will walk the way with us that gets us up the next morning to face the same world we left yesterday. It's support that makes life seem possible, seem doable, when too often all we really want is out of it.

Then it is the spiritual works of mercy that count.

The old spiritual documents call us to "admonish"—to remind or warn or give advice to—the person who cannot break out of chains they have forged for themselves. It is not a call to harsh evaluation; it is about conscious awareness of the problems a person faces. It is about the willingness to stay in the struggle with the one who struggles until, finally, the trap of internal addiction gives way to life again.

The insights and interventions and care we give, when people cannot see their own way out of the quagmire that is themselves, is light in darkness. It is often the one rope they cling to in their desperate attempt to change.

It is a spiritual work of mercy to instruct, to help educate, people out of their ignorance.

It is a spiritual work of mercy to counsel and comfort and forgive with patience, with understanding, with a care that is personal. It is a spiritual work of mercy to identify with the pain of the other, to understand its grip on them. It requires that we can find in ourselves the same persistence the spiritual patient needs to go on trying to cure what will not go away.

It is a long, hard journey out of darkness to a light that has never really been there in the first place.

And the foundation of it all is loving understanding.

Empathy is not harsh evaluation. Empathy is genuine awareness, conscious awareness, felt awareness of the despair that comes with the kind of pain that is impervious to pain. It is the lifeline for those who do what hurts them because they cannot do otherwise.

Sympathy sustains a person through the pain of the moment. It holds a person up until the pain calms, until the pain melts into the normal. But empathy sees into the crevasses pain leaves. Empathy brings understanding of the depth of the pain and the hope for new life that comes with every step out of it. It is, in fact, our own ability to understand within ourselves the extent of another person's emotions that is a measure of our own. To be unable to recognize, to feel, to understand the root of the emotions of another is sign of a stunting of our own.

Scientists call this ability to feel the feelings of the other the result of mirror neuron receptors. Mirror neurons, researchers tell us, reside in the brain of higher animals and fire both when they perform an activity themselves as well as watch it in another. They make empathy possible. Mirror neurons, researchers suggest, are what make it possible for us to identify with the feelings of others. Their joy, their sorrow, their pain, their hopes link with our own strong feelings about the same things and make us one in our desire for their resolution.

Empathy and sympathy are not the same things. Empathy feels the feelings of another. When we see a widow cry at a bedside, when we watch her go home to a penniless family, we feel the emptiness of it, too. When we see the anguish on her face, her dread of tomorrow, her despair for the future, we ourselves feel the great gray wall of life she's facing. We cry the tears we see in her.

Sympathy, on the other hand, feels concern for the person who is suffering, but does not feel the feelings they are feeling. We realize that they are dealing with an overload of feelings they themselves cannot handle. We give them our best wishes and tell them to call us if they ever need any particular thing we can do for them.

Sympathy is a long spiritual distance from the kind of empathy that plunges us into the pit of the person whose feelings demand a response of our own.

THE GOLDEN RETRIEVER

DUFFY IS ADOPTED

Rejection

In some ways, it is easier to describe what Duffy was not, rather than try to tell anyone what he was. He was not a gleeful dog as Danny had been. He was not a rogue of a dog. He was not a scamp of a dog. He was not a mischief-maker of a dog. He was—a shadow of a dog.

Oh, he had a pedigree, all right. A great pedigree. In a sense that I came later to understand, it was precisely his pedigree that destroyed him. He never got to be who he really was, because of who he was expected to be too soon. Let me explain:

We were still grieving the loss of laughing, loving Danny when the call came. A young woman who had visited the monastery over the years had heard about the death of Danny. And then, at about the same time, she came to know, too, of an exhibitor who presented show dogs in competitions. This trainer and dog exhibitor, she learned, intended to have one of her highly bred golden retrievers euthanized. "Strange," I thought and my face must have showed it. "It means 'destroyed,'" she said. "He got too big."

No other explanation offered. This dog had simply had the misfortune to "outgrow the standard of the breed." He was, in other words, too tall or too broad or too something to compete. He had grown beyond the statistics determined by someone, somewhere, to be ideal for golden retrievers. As a result, he no longer qualified to enter dog beauty pageants. He was no good for stud. In fact, he was of no financial good to her at all anymore. He had to go.

Did we want him, the girl on the phone pressed. If we would promise to take him, she was sure she could negotiate some kind of agreement to make it possible. I could hear the urgency in her voice, but for someone who made decisions easily, this one took some doing for me. We weren't over Danny yet. But we did love dogs. The house might not be ready for another dog. But it might be easier to accept when we were used to having one around than it would be later. We had never even seen the dog. But, like all babies, aren't all puppies gorgeous? We didn't have the time to think it through. But if we didn't think quickly, this dog was going to be dead.

I took him.

The agreement was this: First, that we ourselves would never breed him and so taint the line. Second, we would never sell him or give him away. And third, that if we ever did decide to get rid of him, he had to go back to the trainer to "be put down"—the euphemism did not soften the reality for me.

The very thought that I would promise him a good home

and then willy-nilly withdraw the promise appalled me. If we took him, we would keep him. Abandonment sounded just as unethical, just as heartless to me as systematically disposing of him.

I read the agreement with a shudder and put it away where I would never see it again.

When I watched the small car coming up the monastery driveway, I had pictures of a small gold puppy bounding out of it. He would be alive and free in a hundred acres of meadow and creek and woods and rolling green hills. Paradise regained, as the poet said. Bliss.

But it wasn't like that. When the car door opened, nothing happened at all. This great large gold bear of a dog simply stood on the backseat, barely moving, clearly afraid.

Was something wrong with this dog, I asked. No, the girl said, it was just that after he "outgrew the standard of the breed," he was relegated to a dog run rather than the house. She had raised him in the house in order to accustom him to public attention at dog shows, but when it became a waste of time to train him, she put him back outside in the kennel run.

It was not an easy transition. Having once been the crown jewel of the family, he had suddenly become its outcast— forgotten, left alone, and ignored. He was three years old now, fed and housed all his life, yes, but never loved since. What's to trust in a human world like that?

Do dogs get depressed? Whatever the official answer, this one was.

But, oh was he trained! It was almost pitiable to watch him. Call this dog to come and he trundled across the room and threw himself flat on his face in front of you. No joy in coming.

No joy in getting there. He had been robotized to the point of pain. Where was the dog in this dog?

The word "puppy" conjures up an aura of abandon. In our mind's eye we see little explorers sniffing around the house, like babies discovering their belly buttons or reaching for mobiles over a crib. But none of that happened here. At least not quickly. Not soon.

Somehow or other, in anticipation of dog show ribbons and championships, puppyness had been scripted right out of Duffy. We had an old dog, an empty kind of dog, in a young dog who had never really found life for himself. It had been given to him in short phrases: come, sit, down, and stay. All of them are valuable things to know, but all of them, in his case, had been exaggerated to the point of meaninglessness.

This dog looked for a command in every encounter. He didn't know play. He didn't understand tussle. He suspected love. He was afraid to start a tug-of-war. He simply stood in front of me mute, starkly still, and waiting for one more judge in his life to evaluate him. It hurt to watch.

Duffy was a gentle dog, a well-mannered dog, a totally pro-grammable dog. But he was not a happy dog. He lacked a sense of freedom. He seemed wary of real relationships. It didn't matter. You had to love something so noble looking, so pliable, and so deeply wounded. He had never been allowed to become a Real Dog before someone made a Show Dog out of him and left him with only half a life.

My first attempt to free Duffy was to decide that no one who was involved with caring for him would ever give him a command again. It was the one clear gift I could think of to prove to him the trustworthiness of his essential dogness.

"Duffy," I would say silently as I looked into his deep, wise, and knowing eyes, "you are enough just as you are. You have had all the shaping into someone else's expectations that you will get for the rest of your life. From now on, all you need to learn is how to be yourself."

Duffy's rejection cost him an ordinary dog's life. But Duffy's love for others made him almost universally accepted in a way few—either dogs or people—ever really know.

Memories are neither bad nor good. They are simply events logged in the brain that act as markers on our way through life. We remember early birthday parties, for instance, or special Christmases, or the usual rites of passage: graduations and Eagle Scout ceremonies and the death of grandparents and the move to another town. It isn't that whatever happens to us is of unusual significance. Most of what happens to anyone, in fact, is more universal than unique, more run of the mill than astounding, more taken for granted than truly unexpected. But the way we remember them, the feelings that rise in us when we think about each of them, do count a great deal.

Some events simply blend into the mist of life, leaving a kind of quiet glow behind. Others bring as much pain today as they did the day they happened. Maybe more so. Some memories wrap us in a cocoon of security; others open old wounds all over again.

One of most difficult things in life to bear, for instance, is *not* losing the game or making a mistake at the piano recital or being put down in public by the local bully. Even then, down deep we always knew that there would always be other games to play, other opportunities to perform—even more satisfying ones—and other ways to beat a bully.

Incidents like that simply warn us to do better the next time, to be more alert to danger the next time, to be prepared at all times to meet the moment and survive it.

No, the moments that scar the soul, that leave indelible marks that come back over and over again during the years, are the long, slow instances of being rejected by our peers. For no reason of our own making. Without warning. With malice.

A situation like this is not simply the garden variety difficulty of the day, meant to be resolved. Rejection is a great deal more serious than that. This is rejection: it is bare-faced alienation from a society of which we thought we were a part, or certainly expected to be a part, but were denied entry for no good reason at all. Except that we were different. Or new in town. Or perceived to be a threat to somebody else's status in ways we ourselves could never know.

We close down inside ourselves, the nice friendly smile frozen on our face.

Then, rejection breeds an eternal, slow-burning reluctance ever to risk heart, or public face, or my soul to that kind of overt repudiation again.

The childhood scars that come from never being accepted for the team or never being invited to the parties never disappear. And in their place, fear takes over. The fear of ever being so humiliated, so alienated again.

These are people who stop reaching out—for fear of being ignored. They cease to join the crowd—for fear the crowd won't have them. They turn inside themselves and become observers of life rather than its participants.

And so, so many of us fail ever to come into our own. To become all we were meant to be. To grow beyond the pain of childhood rejection or adult failure.

But it is precisely those experiences that limit our social repertoire.

Like Duffy, we learn not to venture out of our approved routines. We make ourselves invisible by never calling attention to ourselves. We hide within the boundaries of social custom and communicate at the lowest possible level. We talk little and say even less, if for no other reason than to make sure that we never say anything of which this particular crowd disapproves.

If we are eternally vigilant, we know, there is nothing they will be able to dispute in us. Nothing of which they can really disapprove. All we need to do is to stay inside the lines and confine ourselves to the routine and we'll be safe.

It is a pathetic way to live a life because it is not really life at all. It is a prison of our own making.

Like Duffy, we learn from rejection to distrust differences—including our own. We never get to the point where, in a group, we can speak up and say, "Well, that has not been my experience" or "I don't see it that way."

We know now that our experience doesn't count and so we suppress it, even to ourselves. Worse, our experience may be exactly what gets us drummed out of this corps, this office coffee klatch, this line for promotion.

To be ourselves, we have come to see, is a very dangerous thing to be.

Finally, like Duffy, all the beauty of our differences, all the spice of our personality, all the talents we never try, all the gifts we never hone, go dry in us. We live a life that is not really alive in us at all.

And it is all wrong.

So what is there to do about it? There are in me two questions that must be answered in order to know what to do about it. First: So what? So this group of neighbors does not accept you for what you are. There are other people out there, doing the things you would like to do, who are just waiting to meet you, to join you, to take you in.

And the second question is: What is the worst thing that can happen if the group you'd like to be in really will not take you in? You'll need to find another job? Another place to live? Another church to go to? Another club to join? Then, the answer to the second question is the first: So what?

The day you expand your own circle and begin to say the things you've been swallowing for years, you will find the groups that want to talk about them. You will begin to free yourself from inside out. You will begin to experiment with the rest of yourself in public. Most of all, you will find the person you have left behind. And best of all, people will love you for it. Different people, of course, but certainly people who themselves know what it is to be a person—and prefer that to becoming cardboard cutouts of a plastic world.

It is when we become ourselves that people have the very least control of us and we have the beginning of the whole of ourselves. Then, like Duffy, we will begin to bloom.

DUFFY'S EARLY FORMATION

Woundedness

Never doubt that early training and formation works—sometimes in our favor, sometimes not. For Duffy, it became a nemesis. Duffy, it seemed, came trained from the whelping box. And the implications of it worked both ways.

From one perspective, the very clear concentration on professional performance in the show ring made Duffy a model of a dog. Erect and attentive, he answered every call. He didn't jump or bound or bark out of time. In fact, he hardly made a sound. If Duffy needed anything in life, he needed a good dose of disobedience. Or a leather briefcase to chew on—as Danny had done with the birthday present I'd been given the year before I'd been given him. At least Duffy could have used a go at digging up the neighbor's new tulip bulbs, just for the sheer joy of knowing the taste of sin. But no, he made the average dog look absolutely criminal.

On the other hand, there were by-products of his early training that limited him all his life. Duffy, we discovered his first night in a new house, had some serious problems to deal with. And so, as a result, did we.

I make a habit of calling home regularly when I'm traveling, and this night was particularly important. How this dog would adjust to new surroundings was anyone's guess. I could hardly wait to call home.

I heard the phone ring and I heard someone answer. But I found the call almost impossible to understand. There was clearly some kind of struggle going on. The voices were indistinct, muffled, shifting from high to low, everybody talking at once.

I could hear the coaxing from hundreds of miles away. Someone clearly thought a piece of meat would do it. No, try a toy, I heard someone else say. Then, I could make out, they were tugging on his collar, trying to get him to test the stairs one step at a time. But nothing, not even the sight of the dog dishes below him, could move him. He simply stood at the top of the stairs, his big bulk stolid, his head drooped, eyes sad, legs shaking, his toenails dug into the long-piles of the carpet. This dog was going nowhere.

Finally, when he inched up to the edge of the stair for one last look at the problem, someone in the group gave a sigh, and played the last card. With someone in front to catch him and someone behind to guide him, she pushed him.

"What's happening?" I shouted down the phone. And then

I understood: the dog was sliding down one step at a time on his big-boned chest. The despair echoed across the miles. Now what was I going to do? I had a dog that simply refused to walk down a set of stairs.

It was only the next day when the real extent of the situation became clear. Duffy would not walk up the stairs, either. Instead, he had to be wrapped in a blanket and, with a person on each corner, dragged all the way up.

How could a young dog, healthy in every respect, be in such a condition? Was this fear? Stubbornness? Neuroticism raised to high art? What could possibly explain the fact that anybody would have a dog they had to carry upstairs as well as down?

The answer covered the range from outlandish to simple: Duffy had, unfortunately, been raised with his talents in mind, rather than his life.

By the time Duffy was weeks old, he had been selected by expert eyes as championship material. He had it all: coat, girth, gait, and docility. He had great potential. He could be an international winner all his life. Better yet, he could become an international stud for years. The financial potential of that for animal owners is near to limitless and definitely not to be ignored.

No wonder then that Duffy would have been taken out of the kennel run for special attention. In this case, that meant inclusion in the family itself. He became the Canine Champion in Waiting. With that expectation, he was under watch twenty-four hours a day, in a one-story home where he could be trained, socialized, and corrected at any and every moment.

The only thing they forgot, apparently, is that dogs also have to learn to crawl up stairs, to jump into cars, to bound down staircases, or to jump over fences. It's the little things that can be so easily missed in life.

But the effects of them last for the rest of life, nevertheless.

"Lead a child up in the way they must go," the old saw teaches us, "and when they are old they shall not depart from the way." The truism is rich in both warning and truth. Our early training counts. It shapes us. It also limits us and challenges us. And the formula matters for animals, too, it seems.

The truth is that, as a result, Duffy never did do steps well, for instance. Nor could he get into the backseat of a car without a boost. Which didn't mean that he didn't love a ride in the car or wouldn't follow you all the way to Nowhere, however many the stairs he would need to climb to get there. He just never did any of those things with ease. Instead, he did them because being with the people he loved was apparently more important to him than being comfortable where he was.

I looked at him often and wondered to myself if I would put as much energy as Duffy did into doing things I could not do, did not feel like doing, did not have the energy to do, did not really need to do. It's doubtful. And yet, it was clear that to Duffy, life was all about being loved, being present, being wanted, being ready. Just in case you got up and went somewhere else, he was prepared at all times to go with you.

In fact, come to think about it, what else is there in life besides people for any of us. And what is it but the care and concern of others that invite us to the fullness of ourselves and are there to applaud us on as we go.

And Duffy repaid me mightily for that gift by giving me his full attention ever after. Unlike Danny, he never ran away, he never left the neighborhood, he never left my side again.

Just being able to be that simple, steady presence was clearly enough for him. And it was a real gift to me.

———

Each of us has been wounded by something on the way through life. No one of us really goes through all of life whole.

In fact, the great Olympic struggle of existence may be exactly our need to work through our wounds to the point of our deepest, most secret valor. Only then, perhaps, can we come to peace with what we have done with the years as we were given them.

It's easy, of course, to dream of doing great things someday— but our greatest gift to others, as well as to ourselves, may well be, in the final analysis, what we have done with ourselves. To grow beyond our limitations as we know them is surely the great task of the human enterprise. Otherwise, what do we have to bring to everything else in life as we go?

The problem is that we have learned to see woundedness as negative. As a drawback. Or an obstacle. Or a curb to success, to the fulfillment of the self. But that is only half the story.

The other half of woundedness lies in its invitation to give our whole selves to something else. It enables us not to squander our lives on multiple things when we can focus our hearts and our talents and our time and our efforts on bringing particular gifts to full bloom.

The story of Tanaquil Le Clercq, considered by many to be one of the most talented ballerinas of the twentieth century, has been memorialized in the documentary biography *Afternoon of a Faun: Tanaquil Le Clercq*. But the film is not really about the dancing of such a talented ballerina. It is about the fact that she got polio at the very acme of her career and never danced again.

It would be a tragic story if it were not for the fact that Tanaquil Le Clercq refused to allow it to be a tragedy. She refused to give in to the limitation. She refused to give up her talent and her love for ballet. She simply reshaped it and in doing that became one of its long-lived artists. She spent years of her life as a choreographer, including with George Balanchine, the genius of ballet, and became a genius of ballet in her own right.

Woundedness is a call to find the rest of ourselves and release it.

There is a deep, deep spirituality in woundedness. It is based on the awareness that the universe is friendly. It allows us to see that life is not meant to be defined by any single dimension of it. Its goodness oozes out of all its pores.

In Tanaquil Le Clercq's case, perhaps only she saw the strange configuration of it. Others would call her career ruined. But every dancer knows that dancing is a very short career in comparison with many. She turned its abrupt wounding into the gift of her life—and one of ours, as well. As do so many whose stories will never be told.

At every turn in the road, at every moment of wounding, we are given the opportunity to find the "More" of ourselves—and, in many cases, what we find is a part of us that we ourselves did not really know was there.

What really destroys the spiritual gifts of woundedness is attitude, not activity. The ability to become our best selves lies in the determination to become what we can be—rather than mourn, regret, resent what we cannot be or do.

It is all a matter of learning to give all of life a chance.

Every change is an opportunity to become something that has been lying dormant in us while we tried to be something else. When we refuse to allow what cannot be to destroy what can be in us, we cut off the coming of a new summer for our souls. We choose the death of an old life to the possibility for a new one.

Woundedness is not the end of everything. It is the beginning of something else, something we would never have dreamed of—unless something else we thought we wanted ended.

DUFFY'S SOCIAL LIFE

Relationships

Life, Duffy knew, could spin like a kaleidoscope and redo in a second everything you thought you could take for granted about it. Worse, you would never know what you had done to deserve it. Or how to stop it from happening again. So Duffy had learned not to approach anyone who did not first approach him.

It wasn't surprising, then, to discover that Duffy lived life very close to the ruff. He didn't bound, as Danny had, into every strange crowd with one of those "Here I am, you lucky world" gestures. That free-form life got Danny into lots of trouble, yes, but it also got him lots of friends. Instead, Duffy—big, beautiful, gorgeous Duffy—hung back. And waited. Your move.

Two of the old nuns were sisters by birth, but you would never have known it. One of them, Sister Thomasine, was a music teacher and outgoing; the other, Sister Bonaventure, had been a high school principal. A formidable one. One of the highlights of their daily schedule, for whatever reason, was to take a trip down the administration hall to see Duffy. You could hear them coming, grumbling all the way: "He won't pay a bit of attention to me," Sister Bonaventure would say. "He always pays attention to me," Sister Thomasine would crow.

Duffy, curled up in front of my desk, raised an eyebrow and waited for the call. "Come here, Duffy," the gruff one would call. And then, "See, I told you he won't come for me." I looked at Duffy beseechingly. Please go and make her day, I begged him with my eyes, but it was clear, he had no intention whatsoever of moving.

Then, the other one called, "Here, Duffy, Duffy, I'm out here. Hurry on." And to my eternal shock, I watched Duffy get up off the rug, nose-open the door, and go right up to the nun, sniffing and pawing and nudging all the way. Impossible, I thought, and frowned at Duffy. This dog was his own worst enemy socially. And he wasn't doing much to buoy up my social index either, come to think about it.

I could hear them bickering about the thing all the way down to the other end of the hall: "I never did a thing to that dog but he won't pay a bit of attention to me," the first one lamented. "You aren't nice enough to him," the second one said.

Years later, Thomasine admitted to me with a giggle that she had come every day with doggy candy in her apron pocket. Of course Duffy responded to her. And Bonaventure, her sister, had never figured it out. Thomasine had apparently let Bonaventure go to her grave feeling rejected by the dog who knew rejection better than anyone in the community.

Obviously, Duffy had learned some things few people give much thought to. Instead of trusting his heart to fair-weather strangers, he was more self-protective. And Duffy learned them the hard way, to such an extent that they colored every relation he had for the rest of his life.

Duffy didn't take people at face value. He wanted to know in every instance what the people themselves intended to bring to their relationship. He had, after all, been totally docile, totally obedient once—and found that submission was simply not enough on which to build a relationship. Now a smarter dog, he wanted to know whether or not the people who called him intended to invest something of themselves in the relationship, as well. Like love, perhaps.

He wanted something out of his relationships now. Not in a selfish way, I don't think. He simply wanted to know that people cared enough about him to give him something for his own sake—as well as to come simply expecting to take something from him, like adoration or obeisance.

From everyone else, he kept his distance.

Duffy had become quite self-contained in his loneliness. He demanded nothing and required little. He could watch people come and go in and out of the office all day long and never growl, or beg, or pester, or be a distraction. He lived well with what he had and selected his friends few and far between. If you didn't like him, he didn't bother you—unlike Danny, who would stay at the person who ignored him until, by dint of beguilement, he wore them down.

Finally, Duffy lived by a hard and rigid rule: he responded to those who reached out to him first. He made no cheap and easy liaisons, no one-night romances, no superficial intrigues, no fly-by-night affairs. Duffy was into his relationships for keeps.

He loved every sister in the office. But he studied every person who came in the door of the monastery and chose his hospitality carefully. Those who had loved him and needed him most, he never forgot. As the wheelchairs and walkers and residents of L'Arche, the Vanier community for the handicapped and mentally challenged, came in the monastery door calling his name, he stood staunchly by. He never withdrew from them. They leaned heavily for balance on his broad shoulders. They sank into his neck with kisses and loving words. They squealed his name from one end of the foyer to the other, and he loved and cuddled and pressed close to each of them. One at a time. These were his friends, the ones he felt loved by, the ones who loved him unconditionally, and the ones he loved and seemed to understand best.

One woman who came to the monastery, interested in religious life but cautious of it, too, was met by Duffy at the front door. "This must be a good place," she thought to herself. "They have a dog." Intimidated by the quiet of the large foyer and aware of an order quite foreign to the world from which she came, she could have walked out, she said later. Instead, thanks to Duffy's welcoming and gentling presence, she came and came and came again—until she finally stayed.

Duffy, it seems, had a sense for what truth and love are actually all about. It is a rare gift and an even rarer reality in a world made of tinsel and trapped in narcissism.

Once we see a relationship disintegrate, one we took for granted, one we felt sure was trustworthy, we are almost required to ask ourselves what a relationship really is. If it can be discarded so lightly, is there anything at the level of human relationships that can be—even should be—trusted at all? And how can we tell?

We live in a thicket of relationships in modern life. It isn't that we have too few; our problem may be that we have entirely too many. The truth is that relationships take an almost absurd number of forms in contemporary society. So many, in fact, that it can be very difficult to understand the distinctions among them.

A "relationship" in this day and age can range from an acquaintance to a love affair, from kinship to friendship, from affinity to intimacy, from cognizance to conversance. From recognition to affection.

But the heart knows better than that.

The heart knows that there are many things that posture as relationships which, if put to the test, disappear like dew on summer grass. It's what does not disappear when darkness comes that really affects our lives. Consistency, understanding, and fidelity distinguish a relationship from an association. It is those things of which a relationship is made.

The differences between them are, in the end, relatively easy to tell. Consistency, understanding, confidentiality, and fidelity are of the essence.

There is some degree of consistency that makes a relationship real. Good friends have a way of being there—not daily, perhaps, but certainly when life demands their presence most. When their presence alone can bring meaning to the moment, they are always there.

Only real friends can really understand the depth of the pain and bring relief. They do not come as gawkers at a tragedy.

They are at its center, bringing its balm, its comfort, its ano-dyne. It is understanding itself that divides the pain, makes grief possible. In front of the friend, there is no need to lie, to hold up like plastic on a stick, to press down the very emotion that is at this time the only proof of the life that's left in us.

Finally, if the relationship is real, then fidelity itself will make the companionship that follows it through both darkness or light, pain or outrageous joy, possible. Relationship takes lone-liness away, makes abandonment impossible, promises life in the midst of death because the heart and the strength of the other enables us to face it.

There is no thought of abandonment where a real relation-ship is concerned. There is only the surety of presence—as long as it takes for us to become fully ourselves again. It is a marriage of the soul and, like any marriage, it is rare to the point of being monogamous. There are few of these in any one life and one of them, in fact, is more than enough.

But this culture does not live on relationships. We live on connections—the people who get us to the next rung on the imaginary social ladder in our heads.

We look for liaisons, rather than relationships. Comfort for the moment will do, rather than comfort that speaks of bond-edness. Anything else speaks of responsibility, of obligations we do not want to assume. In a world where we do not know our next-door neighbors and do not bother to introduce our-selves—because either we or they will be quickly gone some-where else—relationships are better kept bogus.

Our televisions and dating sites and Internet ads sell us romance or, worse, simply the kind of intimacy that wears out quickly and leaves no footprints to itself. These are acquaintances with no phone number, no email address, no time and place set up to meet tomorrow night.

Saddest of all, it seems, are those relationships that are based on a series of short-term affairs in which neither person is interested in more than having a convenient distraction, a comfort station, a release of energy and interest.

In a time of shifting relationships it is narcissism, self-love, and self-interest that drive us to people and then drive us away from them equally easily. The effects of living in a society of serial relationships are many: they create inner emptiness; they choose for connections rather than relationship; they corrupt integrity for the sake of business goals; they erode the sensitivities of the human soul.

These kinds of relationships can divest themselves of people as easily as they divest themselves of animals that cannot bring them ribbons or silver plaques or money. And what it does to animals, it does to us as well: it leaves us wary of the world in which we live and unlikely to trust anyone again.

To have a friend, to create a real relationship, we must be willing to be a friend. Otherwise we are doing what we see people do to animals kept for corporate service rather than kept in the service of the better life.

Our own willingness to bring a steady presence to the life of another—for their sake, rather than only for our own—is basic to the creation of genuine human relationships.

It is a matter of being willing to be there when we're needed, to listen hard and long to hear and understand the underlying pain as well as the particulars of the situation.

Committed to someone for the long haul, there is no difficulty, no amount of criticism or slander or false witness that we will permit them to face alone. Most of all, we go with them not as their lawyer or their debate team or their coach. We do not go with them to strike back. We go with them to be the strength and love and acceptance they need when they feel least cared for by anyone else in their world.

It is that kind of fidelity to the relationship that brings to the other the faith it takes to survive the upheavals, the disasters, the public repudiations of life.

Fidelity does not abandon the friend once they become useless in one area or discouraged in another or sick to heart in a third. Then, at that very moment, is when the relationship becomes real.

DUFFY AND THE
FISH TANK

Insight

———

By now, the picture-perfect personality is beginning to clear:
it's a cameo of Duffy, the stolid; Duffy, the patient; Duffy,
the big, hulking, lovable, quiet one. Duffy was one of those
beautiful pieces of life who could be counted on to be the
same tomorrow as he had been yesterday. No muss, no fuss,
no bother.

All day long, the bulk of him lay inside my office, his nose
and head just breaking the boundary of the room into the hall.
It was a venturesome pose for Duffy when you think of it,
whose idea of daring was to snuggle his head into your stomach
in delicate demand for attention.

But, dull and sedentary as it may have seemed to some, it

had its grace and its gift. People could walk past the office, for instance, without having to worry about Duffy jumping up and leaping into their arms. God forbid that anyone should even think that Duffy would ever jump at all.

He had the bearing of a placid, imperturbable mountain of an animal. Duffy was the veritable living sign of such iconic idols, unfazed, unflappable, and collected. Which, of course, is why what happened later was so shocking, so unbelievably risqué, so refreshingly risqué.

It had already been a long enough day to merit turning out the lights and sinking into the quiet of the evening. But there were guests in the monastery whom I had arranged to meet in the office after evening prayer. It would be a quick and quiet gathering, I was sure. They had crossed the United States comparing this and researching that. Now they wanted the opportunity to air some of their plans with someone who had honest regard for the work but no vested interests in the project.

It was turning into a much longer conversation than I had ever imagined, however. The conversation slipped back and forth between the origin of the project and its public presentation. One good hour of the conversation dealt only with the history of the work and the questions it raised. A second hour concentrated on the political barriers it engendered and a description of the advertising campaign they had designed to promote it. By now, the sun had gone from the monastery courtyard outside the office windows. The room was getting dark.

But if I was getting restless, Duffy was even worse. The dog that never moved began to roll from side to side in the middle of the floor. Legs up, overrrrr and—thump. Then back again: Legs up, overrrrr and—thump.

Then his great square blond head raised up like a mobile camera to scan the room. For a few minutes he lay back down and seemed to relax again.

The light in the room was soft, but the lights on the 40-gallon saltwater fish tank against the wall were becoming brighter by the minute.

Then, unexpectedly, without warning, Duffy leapt up off the floor, shaking and alert, a looming mountain of a dog suddenly possessed by life.

And just as quickly, I became very alert myself. This was a turn of events worth attending to, surely. But what was it?

The company went on talking, oblivious of the earth-shaking changes going on before their eyes. I kept nodding in their direction, but, totally mesmerized by Duffy now, I moved forward in my chair, ready to spring, if necessary. To do exactly what, I did not know, but certainly to save the dog, the company, or the house. From something. Whatever it was.

Duffy was pacing now. His eyes were set on the tank, a shimmering collection of colors, a riot of light. As fish of all colors swam by—tang, wrasse, clown fish, basslets, and dwarf angelfish—the water itself took on the aureola, the nimbus of splendor.

As Duffy began to run back and forth along the edge of the fish tank, the company, too, began to realize that there was something unusual going on. We were now all transfixed by the scene. Me especially. There were forty gallons of water in that tank and it was standing on top of a shelf below filled with hardcover coffee-table books. And the rug was new.

By now Duffy's nose was pressed against the glass of the tank, snuffling and snorting as each little fish went by. He wasn't trying to eat them. He wanted to play with them.

And to make the point, he began to jump up and down a bit, a vain attempt for the kind of attention he had never sought before.

The wrought-iron stand that housed the large tank began to shake a bit and shift and creak. I held my breath. If I grabbed him, he could well pull us both into the unit. If I didn't, in his excitement to get one of the tiny little toy tropical fish, he would surely push it over.

And then, for the first time in his life, Duffy—Duffy!—reared up on his back legs and pressed his paws against the tank. The pressure of his body on the frame was just enough to rock it, certainly enough to upend it when he let go.

But no, after staring at the fish for a good long time, he backed quietly down and off the tank, still stretching to see them all, still enamored of the whole affair.

It was like watching Lazarus rise from the dead. Duffy had been in that office with that tank and those fish for at least two years now. He had never even bothered to glance at the thing, let alone examine it. I could never have had a fish tank with Danny. He would have jumped into the thing.

Not Duffy. Duffy was coming to life, one small part of him after another.

After the event, I thought about it often. It said something to me about human development, about growth, about readiness. Maybe we all come to life only a little bit at a time. Which is why it is well to keep our eyes open for it so we'll be ready when it happens.

Life, we learn as the years go by, is not a free gift. It is given us to grow one piece at a time. And our growing, we soon find out, often comes by inches.

However much we may hope otherwise, life does not happen to us all at once. Sophisticated though we may be, prepared as we are, life has a way of sneaking up on us unannounced and unscheduled. We learn things at different times for different reasons. We think we know what's coming—but we don't. Or, to put it another way, things we have always known we can't know until we live through them. The problem is that we don't apprentice for perceptiveness, let alone for wisdom. We apprentice only for skills. Learning what it takes to be a human, human being, on the other hand, is a process, not an event.

That's why education won't do it. That's why skill is not what it's about. It's easy to teach a person a skill. It is impossible to teach them sensitivity or understanding or perception. We have two tasks: the first is to see life as it is. The second is to understand the rightness of every dimension of it. In the end there is no doubt that everything—death and change, life and growth, pain and joy, love and enmity—are all necessary parts of life. It's learning to cope with all of them that is exactly what being human is really all about.

Time is the one foolproof tool we can depend on where becoming the rest of ourselves is concerned. Given enough time, we will, perhaps, come to appreciate it all. But even time, even the gift of years, is no guarantee that we will see what we need to live life fully—and understand it when it comes. On the contrary, we miss the obvious everywhere. We overlook the signs of new life around us, and think that the only life that's important is what we have within us already. We fail to make room for the life we could have—if we only allowed the vagaries of life to penetrate the Plexiglas behind which we live.

We miss so much of life because we decline to pursue it.

We don't understand hedge funds, for instance, and treat them as someone else's business.

We don't understand the way the prison system works, and so really believe that prison is about rehabilitation rather than incarceration. Then we wonder why so many prisoners go back to prison.

We miss compassion because we have never been poor ourselves, or never had a friend who was poor, or never worked with the poor.

Understanding comes slowly and takes effort that is not there to give when we ourselves are still our one and only subject matter in life.

Life is all about learning to see what we're looking at—if we actually see it at all.

It takes a while, but eventually the really perceptive soul discovers that there are actually five ways of seeing as we go through life.

At the first level of insight, we see only what's in front of us. The immediate becomes the center of the world. We do not see beyond ourselves because we have drawn the circle of life too small, too close, too narrowly. The older next-door neighbor, the colleague with the sick child, the friend whose life is careening off the tracks are part of my consciousness—but not part of my heart.

Their agendas do not compel me to action. Their lives do not really touch mine.

At the second level of insight, we see only the obvious, not what drives the obvious. Not what's under the obvious. We come to see that the other has the same feelings we do and that, like ours, they need to be healed. We see more of the world suddenly, but find it as lonely and confused as our own.

At the third level of insight, we see a broader world, but only from our own perspective. Everyone should live in a democracy, we decide. The whole world would be better off if everyone were like us. We are the acme of the universe, we know. Then, all our efforts go into making the rest of the world like us. Except that never happens and we cannot for the life of us figure out why.

At the fourth level of insight, we see a changing canvas and realize suddenly that nothing is stable, all things are in flux. The question, of course, is whether we realize that we, too, are in the process of change now—because we have seen that nowhere does life stand still.

At the fifth level of insight, we learn to truly see beyond the center of the self and find that we are all alike, all trying to find one another, all wishing to be human together.

At that point, of course, we see our differences and find that they are beautiful—and see our likenesses and discover that they are the stuff of our growth. We do not need to be anyone else now. Instead, we can be everyone else now, understanding them, learning from them—trusting that I can change and become even more of myself at the same time.

The question, of course, is, at what level of insight are we now? What will it take to grow beyond ourselves and discover the rest of life?

DUFFY THE WATCHDOG

Presence

"Is he a watchdog?" one of the visitors to the monastery asked, taking a slight step further away from Duffy's big square head.

I took time to consider the answer carefully. "Well," I said, "the answer is 'yes,' if what you mean by 'watchdog' is 'Does he ever take his eyes off you?' But it's definitely 'no,' if what you mean by the question is 'Would Duffy protect us from the shadows on basement walls?' On the contrary."

In fact, the very thought of Duffy the watchdog reminded me of an old monastic story about two monks who, seeing a dragon in the desert, ran away from it. Then the younger brother said to the old man, "Are you afraid, too, Father?" And the old man replied, "I was not afraid, my son, but it was good for me to run away from the dragon; otherwise, I would not have escaped from the spirit of vainglory."

Oh, the things we tell ourselves to explain our weaknesses, our fears, our limitations, why we are the way we are. I, for instance, told myself lots of things about Duffy: the most important thing was that Duffy was a saintly dog. Oh, sure.

On the other hand, there were other things we knew about Duffy that would be obvious to anyone who had ever been around dogs for a full fifteen minutes. For instance: Duffy was not a dog's dog. No rambling, no growling, no tugs-of-war over Frisbees here. Instead, Duffy would simply lie on the rug in front of the desk and wait. Wait for someone to walk down the hall and call his name, the sure sign of a treat. Wait for me to move out from behind the desk to get a book so he could walk with me from here to there. And back again.

Duffy was most meant, I always thought, to be one of the sitting marble lions on the ramparts outside the New York Public Library—fierce-looking and frozen in cement—than he was ever meant to be a rolling, yelping dog. Sticks didn't much interest him. He might chase one for a time or two, but he never nagged or barked and teased for the game the way most other dogs did. Frisbees were more a source of wonder to him than enthusiasm. He would loll his large head from side to side, following the arc of the disk through the sky with the same kind of stoic magnetism with which he did everything else. Then he dropped his head on his paws once more and went back to waiting, who knew for what?

On the other hand, Duffy had virtues hardly imagined in dogs. Duffy, for instance, was not the kind of dog that barked every time people walked by the door. No jumping on the back of the couch to bark and bang at the windows when cars went by. No crawling over the front seat to growl and wail and yelp and squeal at people simply waiting on a street corner for the light to turn green.

He was nothing but a great friendly bear of a dog who even salivated slowly.

Duffy was patient. All right, be picky: phlegmatic. You couldn't much excite him and, trust me, he did not try to excite you. He had grown into an imitation of a dog who looked like a golden retriever. "Come on, Duffy . . . Come on" brought a lazy look down the hall—if you were lucky—but not much more. Travel, adventure, excitement were not his lusts. He didn't squeeze past guests to fly out the front door. Fly? The very thought of it.

Instead, Duffy's big, soft, loving self could sit in front of me, square head heavy on my thigh for hours, an absentminded ear massage more than enough reward. He was worth his weight in composure, in diligence, in humility. Whatever he was, he was happy to be. Whatever he wasn't, he willingly bore. It was home he wanted and it was love that drove him. Not bravado. Not heroics. Just long-suffering love.

"Long-suffering love" to Duffy meant the willingness to do what he did not want to do—if doing it meant he could be with you.

If you wanted Duffy to take a long walk with you, for instance, he'd go, but only if he could race far enough ahead to be able to lie down and wait for you to get there.

If you wanted Duffy to go for a drive with you, he'd go as far as the car. The cue was for you to pick him up—all eighty-five pounds of him—plant his front paws on the backseat and then, your arms under his back legs, hoist his back end up until he was balanced enough to scoot the rest of the way across the backseat on his two front legs. And then he would sit there all the way to Illinois, if necessary, and never make a sound. Just to be with you. Sigh.

It was the day we got to the rest stop on I-80 in Ohio that life got dicey, when having a waiting, watching, patient, loving, long-suffering honey bear of a dog began to show some downsides.

Designed to be one of those pit stops you see NASCAR doing with such flourish, we came darting into a parking spot closest to the door. We could still conceivably make the meeting on time, but only if we hurried. "I'll go straight into the ladies' room," she said. "You take Duffy into the doggy yard." And then she was gone.

I swept open the back door with a garnish of jollity. "OK, Duffy, heeereeeee we go." Duffy stared after Maureen, didn't give me so much as a nod. "Come on, boy. Over here." I reached for his collar and gave a tug on it. He pulled even tighter toward the door on the other side of the car. "Duffy, please," I pleaded. "We're in a hurry. Come on!" Nothing to do now but pull him over to my door by both legs. He slipped over the edge a bit clumsily. One-third of the enterprise accomplished. We were, after all, out of the car.

Unfortunately, I had failed to assess the rest of the experience.

The doggy yard was a fenced-in area to the right of the rest station. The fragile slats of the orange snow fence, left over from years of lake-effect storms, swayed first one way and then another. It marked off the animal relief area, yes, but this was not Fort Knox.

I could see from where I stood that there was already a man walking another dog inside of it. If big, lumbering Duffy so much as leaned against a slat, that pet area would become an instant open-air reservation.

Then, when I got up to the fence itself, things got even worse. I had seen the man's head above the fence; I had not seen the dog he was walking behind. Let's just call that dog "The Terminator" for short. Because he was short. Very short. A cross between a toy terrier, a Mexican Chihuahua, and a bull-mastiff. But Duffy, unknowingly, walked through the slatted half-open gate.

And then it happened. Duffy attacked the little dog? Not even remotely possible! The little dog, however, reared up on its three-inch legs, gave a sound like the hiss of Niagara Falls, and lunged.

Duffy may not have been any kind of retriever genius, but he was not anybody's fool. And he definitely did not have a death wish. The pivot took me off guard completely. I saw the leash disappear between my legs and the fence bend to the ground. Duffy was careening across the parking lot and with one leap slammed onto the backseat, splayed and dazed a bit.

"How'd it go?" I heard her say behind me. "Fine. Fine," I said. "Let's just get out of here before that other dog calls the cops."

No, Duffy was no watchdog. Unless, of course, you do mean that he only had eyes for you. But that quality in a dog I'll take anytime to a hundred "Terminators."

In a world where cities easily reach populations of millions, "presence," it would seem, is a quality in great supply. After all, people are everywhere: they crush into elevators, work in businesses that easily employ hundreds of people or even thousands. In the apartment next to us neighbors live who we never even see, let alone been introduced to. Even areas of the country that not too long ago were villages are now "bedroom communities," an hour or so outside the city.

Commuters, they call them, and housing developments that city workers empty out of in the morning and escape to when the workday is over. Or, conversely, we simply move from city to city chasing the next job, while our children grow up with friends they will never see again.

It is a crowded, lonely world. Never have we needed presence—the physical contact of old friends or treasured companions—more. Grandchildren grow up on Skype now, and summer "vacations" are a circuit of drop-in visits to old friends and dispersed family outposts we would otherwise never see. Homesteads have disappeared. Sunday dinners with extended family are memories of another era. Larger areas are great culture centers where social "contacts" have taken the place of the weekend card game.

People "exercise" now; they don't sit on the front porch and just talk to people as they go by anymore. In fact, the front porch itself is largely an anachronism. Now "home" is a series of high-rise buildings with fake frontages of empty wrought-iron balconies no one sits on.

Where there are fewer people—or maybe precisely because there are fewer people—people tend now to live alone, most of them denizens of what was once the family home. They get their meals-on-wheels now from gentle strangers who deliver them in private cars and deposit them inside the screen door. They pay their bills on computers. They order their meds online. They go to the clinic where a cadre of doctors rotates hours.

At the end of the day, no one sees them, even fewer know them. They talk to their TVs and their animals—old dogs, stray cats, a few birds.

With all our social media, all our transportation facilities, all our charm courses, presence is far too often a thing of the past now. We hurry through life, heads down, preoccupied and on our way to somewhere else. The person in front of us at the counter, the corner, in the car beside us in the next lane, is more a ghost of a life than a life.

So what's missing? Easy: the lack of real human, really caring, authentically involved human presence. We are becoming a world of cardboard figures, entombed in technology, living on hermetically sealed personal planets. We don't really know anybody anymore, and nobody really knows us.

Social psychologists study the effect of organizations on individuals and individuals on organizations. Their conclusions are clear: they tell us that human behavior is a response to the social climate in which it exists. Both being alone and being with others affects our own human development.

There are a lot of things we can do for other people, like mowing their lawns, or dropping off their mail as we walk by their desks, or bringing a cup of hot coffee from the coffee-maker on cold winter days. But all of those things can conceivably be done by machines, as well. The really important things, the human things—like personal attention, human interest, and meaningful communication—can only be gotten from another human being.

We look for comfort from our friends. We get security from

the family members who check on us regularly. The people who invite us for Thanksgiving and a day on the beach make us feel like valued human beings.

Most of all, the people who sit and listen to us, who care about our life stories, who go out of their way to read our latest medical report or take us for the long-term treatments meant to keep us alive are the ones, we know, who really care for us. They understand the pain and set out to lessen it. They know our needs and, without a word, meet them.

They comfort us in our grief, sustain us in our fears, uphold us through our transitions, and help us begin the long, hard trek up the gorges of life to start all over again.

Without them, we bear the weight of isolation alone. We stumble through the dark parts of life. We lose our way and lose the models we need to tell us that life has not ended, only changed. We go numb to the center of our souls, and the atrophy of worthlessness and lovelessness sets in.

DUFFY ON THE LAKE

Diversity

Beginning in the nineteenth century in Scotland, the golden retriever was bred to be a bird dog. The dog's value was in his breeding as a retriever on land—and in water. At least I believed that once. Until Duffy came.

It was the year I could hardly wait for summer to come. Duffy and I had bonded very well. He stayed by the office during the day; I kept him in my bedroom at night. I could open the door to let him out and he never ran away. He came at every call. Here was the perfect dog for the perfect afternoon. Now was time for the fun part.

As June melted into July, I made elaborate plans. We would go to the lake for a day where his double-layered deep golden coat would keep him warm in the water and cool in the sun. I'd do all the doggy things with him: the Frisbee for the campgrounds and a stick for the water. I'd put a tennis ball in the bag just in case he wanted to chase it as he swam. This was going to be a really fun day. A whole group of the sisters had gathered to watch this large, gentle dog—who was so constrained in his actions—be free to churn up the lake if he wanted to, no limits given, no amount of swimming too much swimming.

On the trip to the water, Duffy sat in the backseat of the car, protected by his usual disdain for anything as mundane as excitement. He was as calm as ever, totally unflappable, barely bothering to notice the number of toys in the basket next to him. And, once parked in the lot, we had to coax him out of the car as usual.

But once on the bluff above the beach, Duffy changed. He began to pant a bit and run around in circles. My fear, of course, was that he would simply go charging into the water before any of us could get in there with him. I wasn't worried about him, but I was concerned that he might go out further than any of us ought to venture. The lake bed was uneven and deeper in places than I would want anyone to go who wasn't a natural swimmer.

So, I rushed down the hillside ramp to the beach, calling for Duffy all the way and fully expecting that he would be on my heels in seconds. But when I turned around, the dog who always came when called was nowhere in sight. I caught my breath. He must have gone by me so fast that I never saw him.

I scanned the water for sight of his bobbing head. There was nothing in sight.

This time, I looked back up the hill for him instead of down the beach. No Duffy there, either. I walked back up the ramp.

And there he was, settled down in high grass, chewing on strands of straw, and completely settled in for the afternoon.

"Duffy," I called, "come on. We're going swimming. Come on! Duffy, don't stay there. Duffy!" But Duffy never moved.

I got out the Frisbee and rolled it across his nose down the bluff. Duffy never moved. I went over and tugged on his collar. Duffy played dead dog and slumped over on his side, like a sack of wet cement. Completely uninterested, totally blasé. Oh, great.

Getting him down the ramp was another story. He lowered his head and dug in his feet so that as we pulled him you could hear his feet scrape along the pebbles. Maybe this wasn't such a good idea? Except that he was a water dog, after all, and at least deserved the right to do what such breeds loved best. Nothing about the rest of his life seemed to be much fun.

The jump to the beach at the end of the ramp wasn't all that high, but Duffy balked again. This was not a dog that rushed headlong and reckless into life. This one calculated—and then, after deliberating, decided to do just what he had refused to do in the first place. In one swift motion, we found ourselves right back again to his first night in the house with the stairs: calling, pleading, coaxing.

The angle of the ramp gave us all the momentum we needed. The next thing I knew we were splashing in the water, face down and swimming. When I came up about ten yards out, got my footing and turned around, I knew instantly that something was wrong. And sure enough, there was Duffy, going exactly the opposite direction from the rest of us and churning full steam ahead back to the beach.

I tried the stick. I threw the ball. I splashed and called and splashed some more. By this time, Duffy was long out of the water and trying to scratch his way up the hill.

I began to laugh out loud. Somewhere I had seen the *Peanuts* cartoon I should have known about before Duffy came: Frame one: The man throws a stick, saying as he does, "I the man shall throw this stick for you the dog." Frame two: The stick flies through the air. Frame three: The stick flies through the air. Frame four: The stick falls to the ground unnoticed and Snoopy, propped up and typing on his typewriter, writes, "And I the dog could not care less."

I got it. It was the lesson of a lifetime: The expectations we have for another will not change either their basic interests or their basic abilities. The individualism that is their gift to the world must not be denied. And the error is not theirs, it is ours. We can't make anyone else be what we want them to be—but we can let them be themselves, and love them for that and that alone.

———

The world runs on stereotypes, all of them false, all of them useless. Some of them even dangerous. And yet we persist, to our own peril and to theirs.

We stereotype people, and we do it with impunity. "Women," we say we know, "are weak and emotional," "Germans are soulless and efficient," "Russians are dour," "Americans are loud," and "Muslims are terrorists."

We say all these things with such certainty, such unmitigated gall that it takes on the aura of divine truth. It makes a lie out of everything else in life. It brings us all to human ruin.

We build armies around stereotypes and so deny our own

children the resources, the education and food they need to grow. How many others will need to die before our fears are allayed and our stereotypes can no longer be justified?

Indeed, Germany ran itself into oblivion as a result of its militarism. The Soviet Union collapsed under the weight of its militarism. Now the United States is struggling to manage a budget and a debt driven by militarism while its infrastructure disintegrates and present needs go unaddressed.

Yet, if that is the ultimate global price of stereotyping, it has an even more toxic effect on the individual soul. When we live in a box made out of our clichés and prejudices and the rapacious fears they breed, we limit the stretch of our minds. We pollute the texture of our souls.

When we begin to see people as "types" rather than as individuals, we cut ourselves off from reality. We fail to find out for ourselves exactly what this particular person is like, or feels, or wants, or would be willing to die for. It is a world lived in a black bottle where we make up—out of nothing but our mental fantasies—what the world actually looks like.

Lack of outreach in the human life smothers the human soul. We forget how to love, we fail to risk love, we destroy the seeds of love by refusing to nurture them. We wall ourselves off from excitement and experience. We see other cultures as inferior and lose the thousands of years of wisdom they bring with them.

Or we wall our cities off into ethnic neighborhoods where the food smells different but we never venture into them to try it. The language sounds different so we miss the power of its poetry, the depth of its lilt, the spirituality of its sources. In the end, all we have managed to do is to miss good food and fresh ideas. We never hear the powerful poetry and great music and the rendering of this one same world in ways that bring new and vibrant color to our own.

We become spiritually lame, limping along on only one rendering of creation and Godness and life. We cripple our souls and blind our eyes and stop up our ears. Most pathetic of all, we forget to wonder how it is that we became so incarcerated in our own prejudices.

Stereotypes and prejudices make for a very lonely, very fraught, very vanilla life. I remember my first time in the Republic of Ireland: suddenly, in the middle of one of my early dinners out, I looked around the dining room with a jolt. "Every single person in this room," I thought to myself, "is Catholic. How boring."

But diversity and pluralism, what we learn from the other, can only bring new depth and meaning to what our own culture has to give us. It also enables us to test the truths we live on, many of which have been distorted by our own extremists, our own guerrillas, our own one-eyed kings. All of whom strive to entrap us in our own small fiefdoms.

The situation is a fatal one. When we live off old errors instead of diverse viewpoints, we deny ourselves the truth and poison the very society we seek to save. We limit our own scope in the world. We condemn our hearts to death and our souls to dust.

We retreat into a cave full of other people's ideas and live there with none of them tested—but all of them declared true. That kind of thinking dwarfs our souls, reduces the options of whole groups in a society and, history is clear on this, ruins one country after another. It is not a pretty picture.

The world needs better of us. We simply cannot—must not—attempt to make the rest of the world into our own cloth. We have too much to learn from them, if only we would open our eyes to it. We all do the same things: community, family, economy, religion, society. But some of us do some of them better than others do. Better than we do.

The world, it seems, could be a more peaceful place. It may be simply a matter of beginning to reach out—one at a time—to the unknown other in our building, on our block, in our city. Then, one person at a time, we can make them friend while letting them be exactly who they are, at the same time. Then, one morning we will all wake up and realize that the world is not only clearly at peace, but that it was we who made it so.

DUFFY AND THE BUTTERFLIES

Beauty

Monasteries are paradisiacal places for animals. Almost everywhere, great monastery buildings sit in the middle of wide open spaces, manicured lawns, flower beds of immense proportions, flowing meadows and woodlands within reach. Ours is no exception.

Deer play in the sunlight behind the dining room for all to see. They parade their young with confidence and graze forever, it seems, to the delight of visitors from the city who watch them from windows less than thirty yards away. The herd moves up and down the tree line slowly. With dignity. No fear here. No sense of tension. They simply live among us with a security seldom seen in their kind, on property they seem to intuit is marked "No Hunting."

In this place, the two species go together easily, with respect for each other, and with a gentle sense of belonging together.

Large king salmon spawn in the creek that runs through the monastery grounds to the lake. Small animals—squirrels especially—live in every tree. And there, in the midst of that Eden, sat Duffy, king of the mountain, imperial looking and resplendent in the midst of it.

The only problem was that for Duffy, "sat" was the operational word. Duffy didn't revel in the place and careen through the property, head up and ears flying like Danny had done. No electricity ran through his veins at the sight of a row of willow trees bent and arching. No howls came out of him as a gaggle of geese flew overhead. No lust to simply run away into the woods ever captured his heart and set his feet flying.

Duffy would do a lap or two around the large front lawn and then simply slump to the ground to survey his property. He particularly liked to go outside with someone, rather than alone, and was perfectly happy simply to follow them from point to point, for no sure reason at all.

Duffy you could depend on simply to stand guard over all of life with great aplomb and no hint of hysteria whatsoever.

But one day, to my amazement, all of that changed.

I was sitting at my desk when the word came: Duffy was outside but "acting very strangely."

By the time I got to the front door, I could see him in the distance, head down, smelling his way along a trail of some sort, I supposed. So what was wrong with that?

Until I saw his head jerk up and snap around. His body

seemed to pitch forward, and then tighten and tremble a bit. With one last halting kind of leap, he seemed to lick at the sky in one final, fruitless effort. Then he fell back stock-still and waited for the ballet to start all over again.

By that time, I could hardly breathe just watching him. It must be a convulsion, I said. I had heard about dogs having seizures but I had never seen one—and I certainly did not know what to do about it if it were one. If I ran toward him and frightened him into another spasm, perhaps he would die. If I tried to grab him and he struggled, given his size, we could both be hurt. If it was rabies and he had gone mad, I could be endangering other people as well.

Maybe just standing calmly was the best thing. I stood there quietly, wanting him to see me and be assured. I wanted to allow this moment to play itself out, hoping he would exhaust himself and give me enough time to call the vet.

Then, the strange behavior started all over again. I moved quietly and almost motionlessly toward him. Just a little at a time. Just a foot or two per step. There was nothing to rush about. On the contrary, the more tired he got, the better.

It took at least twenty minutes. I had timed every move to coincide with his own in order not to alert or alarm him, but I was almost there now. Duffy, on the other hand, was deeply involved, totally concentrated on something on the ground, and hardly aware I was even there.

I was almost behind him when I finally got a glimpse of what was going on: Duffy was smelling the flowers. Correction: Duffy was smelling the flowers and chasing the butterflies that were in them. When the butterfly moved, he jerked. When it flew around his head, he jumped. With the butterfly gone, he bent his head into the flowers again, took a long breath, and then waited for the next one to move.

My heart gave a great internal laugh. Duffy was smelling flowers? In the very middle of an ordinary day, he had discovered flowers and butterflies and was having the time of his life with both.

Duffy had discovered what most people I knew had not: there are times in life when what we are doing that is out of the ordinary is far more important than what we should be doing of our ordinary little human things. It is at those moments that we sink into the elixir of life. Then we become one with nature. We are suddenly more than ourselves and life is more than simply a canvas on which to do human things. We feel another part of ourselves and of the world come alive. We begin to feel the beauty within us.

Those moments, in fact, may be the very moments when we really see life for the first time. More than that, these may be the very moments when we are most alive ourselves.

———

Confucius may have said it best: "Everything has beauty," he taught, "but not everyone sees it." Seeing it, the spiritual person knows, is the task of a lifetime. It is also the reward of a lifetime well lived—lived in balance, lived from the inside out as well as from the outside in.

Unfortunately, this culture does not teach beauty in its schools nor require it in its programs. Most of all, it does not prescribe it for its healing value. The value of beauty in shaping the soul, let alone in curing the ills that a lack of beauty brings on, we ignore.

In a plastic world, frenzied by its pursuit of money or dried to the bone by the lack of it, the whole of life is cheapened, devalued. Then the collectibles of life take precedence over its joys. Striving trumps achievement. Nothing is ever enough. Only consumption brings a sense of success in life.

And so life goes by, a merry-go-round of toys gotten or yet to get. Just for the sake of having them. Whether they bring anything of internal value in return is seldom factored into the equation.

And so, in a culture of things, great works of art get reduced to paint by numbers. Buildings are built to storehouse things, rather than as cathedrals of poetry in stone. Things simply come and go, a mass production of bling, bringing nothing but a desire for more.

Without obeisance to the God of More, materialism says, how can we ever say that life has been worth it? How else will we come to know that life has value in itself? How will we ever learn that life lived in pursuit of beauty has been lived beautifully? How will we ever realize that life is about more than engorging ourselves on a multiplication of indigestible things?

Too often beauty, the proof that all things in right balance bring another dimension, another kind of vitality to life, goes undefined as a spiritual value. We miss the obvious: beauty is meant to enable us to transcend the mundane, to escape the frivolous, to save us from the toxicity of the cheap and tawdry.

Because of beauty, we may finally begin to see that the very purpose of life is to make beauty possible. Beauty brings peace to the soul and satisfaction to the heart. It is the very magnet of the soul.

Beauty, the right order of things—the marriage of color and

shape, materials and function—calms the spirit. It saves us from the stress that cacophony brings. It subdues the feverish need to purge ourselves of anything frenetic in a culture that keeps the soul at white heat.

In an age of cheap trinkets and empty action, the soul is easily fatigued by the noise of it all, the emptiness of it all, the pointlessness of it all. Life becomes a round of parties and shopping carts, of fast automobiles and dull talk. Nothing seeds the soul with fresh ideas and new vision. It is all just more of the same, recycled in new forms and places and dates, over and over again.

Then, time in an art museum—just sitting in front of one of the masters—or listening to a symphony can refresh the soul. Then a riot of tulips or crown vetch on a highway bypass can lift our hearts out of the doldrums of dullness that sameness brings.

When every store window satiates the public with nothing but variations of what is being sold by the store next door, having what everybody else has becomes unduly important. It is not about having your own snatch of beauty at hand.

To be enriched by beauty is to have within us the sight of life that will never go away, that will never leave us empty. It is the sight of one single sunset over the Caribbean that brings layers of life to every sunset anywhere in the world ever thereafter. It brings layers of beauty to scenes of pain solemnly endured in some of the poorest places in the world.

To pursue beauty wherever and however it comes—in one solitary rose in a golden vase, perhaps—deepens our consciousness of beauty everywhere and anywhere. We begin to recognize beauty on the faces of the wise and patient elderly. We come to see beauty in the eyes of young foals alive with life and raring to go. We watch beauty break out of every living thing and suddenly realize that the beauty we have found is now in us, too.

Finally, beauty brings us the perspective that comes from being able to separate the cheap from the singularly over-whelming. We begin to watch for it closely where it cannot usually be seen: in the center of one flower at a time, in the soft flutter of an orange monarch butterfly, in the common places where we ourselves live.

When we begin to recognize beauty, to see it all around us, it has done its work on us. Steeped in beauty, we have become beautiful ourselves. We are calm now, uplifted, enriched by the world around us, deepened in our sensitivities, our vision of the world more finely honed. We become the beauty we have come to see everywhere.

Once we begin to chase butterflies and smell flowers, noth-ing in the world can possibly be made to appear more valuable, more priceless, more precious. Then we, too, have become one with the universe, impervious to anything less, fearless in our pursuit of it.

THE CAIQUE

LADY THE COMPANION

Change

With both big dogs gone, the terrible truth dawned. Big dogs age. And when that happens, they need to be carried places. They need to be lifted up the stairs or hauled down them. They must be helped through doors and nursed in chairs. The implications of all that had to be faced. And dealt with. Our days of owning big dogs, however much we would have liked to find another, were clearly gone forever. For the dog's sake and for ours.

So, it was quiet and empty around the house for a good number of years. Then, one day, I saw three beautiful birds, conures, and remembered again all the years I spent with nothing but a little blue parakeet for company. It had been a delightful time.

So now, years later, my mother's good sense about all of those things began to make a new kind of good sense. There are more ways than one in life to deal with reality.

And that's where Lady Hildegard came in. Or almost.

Lady herself, you see, followed another loss. Bennie the little conure came first and then, just like Billy, simply disappeared one day. We think she must have slipped out a door looking for some of us and never found her way back in. It was November, the week before Thanksgiving, cold—too cold outside for a house bird to survive it—and she was so small.

I put up pictures of her on telephone poles and took out ads, promised a reward and sent children around the neighborhood in search, but there was not a sign of her anywhere. Same story, same heartache.

"Come out," Bennie's breeder said when she heard about the loss. "I have a bird I want you to see." I could hardly stand the thought of it. "No," I said, "I really don't want to see any more birds. Ever again."

"Don't say that," the breeder said. "You love birds. Just come out and let them comfort you."

We made the trip to the other side of the city in dark, cold rain. I didn't feel good about the trip. Even if I liked what I saw, I could not bear the idea of starting all over again. It was no time to be outside for anything, I thought, let alone a bird. Until I saw her.

Lady Hildegard—Lady, as she has come to be known—was four months old and weighed about five ounces. She would be a medium-sized parrot, the breeder said, and was already twice as large as Bennie had been.

But most of all, she was stunningly beautiful. A caique, native to South America, she had all the colors for it: bright orange pantaloons on her legs and an orange scarf around her neck, even brighter yellow markings on her white breast, effervescent green wings, a bold black cap on top of her head, and eyes like pieces of amber.

"Hold her," the breeder said. "She's a companion bird." But I hesitated. Anybody with any experience with birds at all knows that you need to work your way into their trust. And, at the same time, you have to work them into being comfortable with your presence, your voice commands, and certainly your hands. Very cautious now, I frowned a bit. "No, take her," the breeder said. "She loves people."

Lady ran up my arms, rubbed her head across my cheek, and surfed down the front of me. Then she grabbed onto my fingers, licking and tasting as she went, learning everything there was to know about me that meant anything to her: she clearly wanted someone who would be soft with her, accepting, and patient. Definitely patient. It seemed a fit.

But most determinative of all: She had been born on July 10, the anniversary of my final profession and First Vespers of St. Benedict's day. What's more, we got her within weeks of the elevation of Hildegard of Bingen, a Benedictine nun, to the status of Doctor of the Church. She was clearly meant to be a Benedictine bird. My Benedictine bird.

So, with Bennie still very present to me, and feeling a bit disloyal at the very thought of putting another bird in her cage, I crafted a deal: if Bennie came home within the next month, the breeder and I agreed, I would return Lady.

Or at least I thought I would. Until I got to know Lady.

We bundled Lady up against the sharp autumn wind and took her out into the dark. There would be chaos in the car,

I knew. Everything in her life right now was new and frightening. She was with strange people outside the house and being moved from one place to another in the dark. These were not small things for a tiny bird to negotiate. I expected hysteria, anger, self-defense, fear. Nothing short of total resistance. After all, these things take time. However, there was really no gentle way to get her home except to put her in the car, however frightening it would be for her, and take her there. We put the heater on high, started the motor, and inched out onto the wet, black highway, both of us holding our breath.

I could feel little Lady squirming inside the blanket and prepared myself for the worst. She might drop onto the floor where I couldn't see her. Or she might bite anything within range. Or she might jump from me to the driver and then we could be really in trouble. Instead, she simply popped her little head up out of the cover I had her cloaked in and took a long, solemn look at everything. The lights of oncoming cars mesmerized her for awhile. But then, eventually, she tired of those, curled up against my neck, and went to sleep. Clearly, this companion bird had found herself a companion—and so had I.

———

Life without change, we know, is dead or deadening. But, never doubt it, change itself can be seen as deadly, too.

Change takes life and tosses it upside down. What was, much as we may have wanted it gone, is no more. Which may be fine at one level, but at another we also know that with this loss goes the loss of everything good that went with it. The familiar, with all its comforts and regularity, disappears. We are left in a maze in the dark to find our ways through to a new life, new relationships, a life without maps and charts to guide us.

To relish life-giving change—the kind that freshens the soul or satisfies long-desired hopes—is one thing; to suffer integral change is entirely another.

The very thought of total dislocation terrifies us. Refugees walking through the desert, with burned-out villages behind them and nowhere to go in front of them, become icons of our own fears.

A new job means new connections to be made, new successes to be racked up. We may not have liked the last institution we were in, but at least we knew how to navigate it. We knew who to ask for what. We knew what it took to move up in its hierarchy. We knew what approval looked like there. But now, darkness is the color of the day and the finish line has disappeared entirely.

A new school means there are no friends to walk home with anymore, no established faculty support.

A new neighborhood means the loss of social networks, however beautiful the new one. We don't know now who will loan us a snowblower in a storm. We don't know who will be home to give us eggs if we need them at the last minute. We don't know who to ask about new doctors and dentists and bus routes. We don't know the streets and the people, the social centers and the stores.

Newness wipes the slate clean. In a society in which everyone else already knows the routes and the social network and the unspoken rules of the system, we are the isolates.

It's not something we choose easily. Moving life from one place to another is a huge decision.

It means watching all the anchor points of life dissolve before our very eyes. Who can possibly know the panic of it until you've been through it? And even then, the feeling never goes away of being foreign, being the outsider, being just slightly out of kilter at all times.

But there are less physical changes that are just as hard on us. Losing a friend can tear the very fabric out of our lives. Losing a spouse can leave us feeling abandoned and rudderless. Losing status can leave us feeling cut off from all the phone numbers we have known in our entire lives.

The bleakness that comes from great change cannot be dispelled. It can only be lived through. Endured. Unless, or until, we begin to realize that jarring change is also a thunderous call to personal development—unsought, yes, but otherwise unlikely. Change expands the horizons of the human heart.

There is something we are being offered that is meant to find the more of us inside of us and let it free. For though we have lost all the markers of our life, we have also been liberated from them.

Now is the time to reshape not just the way we live, but the way we look at where we are, as well. We're free now to be the person we've always wanted to be, but could not possibly allow ourselves to try. The children are gone, yes, but so are the bills with them. So is the driving time it took to get them to all their own life obligations. Which means it is time to decide what new things to put in place of old ones—so we can finally become the rest of ourselves.

It is only ourselves that is holding us back. And that is the most frightening fact of all. Coming to know ourselves again is one of the great gifts of change—the least wanted, perhaps, but, at the same time, surely the most developmental.

It means that we can now review everything in our lives: We can rethink the attitudes we've brought with us from one place to another over time. We can examine the ideas we bought along the way without every really unearthing the roots of them. We can explore the prejudices we've cherished for so long—without an iota of data to make them real—and test them against the new realities around us.

We are being given a chance to begin again. What greater gift can life ever give us?

Change calls for gratitude for the past and trust in the future. It calls for letting go of the chains that have bound us and for testing every possibility along the way. Change means we can try what we've never tried before and find out how much we love it. Or we can become what we were never able to be and realize that all of life has been leading us to this very moment.

Change is not the enemy; change is the opportunity to live again, to live newly, to live without having to bear the burdens of disapproval we have left behind.

LADY AND HER TOYS

Materialism

"Herself," as the Irish say of the woman of the house, established her kingdom quickly. This was clearly not a parakeet, this was a parrot, and whether anyone else knew the difference between the two was totally irrelevant. She did. This was the leader of the flock, the king of the hill, the queen of the court, the owner of the house. Correction: the owner of the owner of the house.

I was certain that it was supposed to be the other way around.

Lady is not lacking in self-confidence. She's not lacking in chutzpah, either.

When I got Lady, I went strictly by the book. And there are many of them—which in itself ought to tell you something about what it takes to own a parrot. One thing was obvious: You don't give parrots orders. You negotiate with them. You decide how you're going to raise her—and she negotiates you out of it.

The first major decision is what to put in the cage.

The books instruct parrot owners to get lots of toys and rotate them. In order to develop properly, parrots need the mental stimulation toys bring, they say. And besides, parrots bore easily.

I'm not exactly sure what they mean when they talk about "mental stimulation." If pulling out the cage tray on her own and unscrewing the wing nuts that hold up her perches have anything to do with it, Lady's had it. She doesn't really need any more "mental stimulation" than she's got. But we go out and get the toys anyway. See what I mean? It's her house, and she is in charge of all of it.

The results are not what I expect. "Foraging toys"—toys that enable a bird to find her own food, as she would need to do in the wild—are big on the list. They come in all sizes and shapes and materials. So, we get one of each: the bell-and-rope kind to chew on, the piñata type to play with, and the plastic problem-solving kind if you're really serious about this foraging thing.

Watching Lady deal with each of them was a lesson in itself. For owners, that is.

The rope kind she swung on for awhile and then ignored it.

The piñata she devoured in twenty-four hours. It was a brightly colored plaited donkey, large and complete with reins and saddle. She grabbed at the reins and sat in the saddle and we have pictures to prove it. And after that, in one day, that was the end of the piñata.

The plastic problem-solving sort of foraging toy, however, was a different experience entirely.

We have had a number of them. This first consisted of four clear plastic boxes, each of which came with a different lid. To get the treats inside, Lady had to figure out how to open each lid differently. One of the four lids she would need to pull toward her. One of them she would need to swing open on a pin. The third required her to slide it off the top of the box. And, to get the fourth lid open, she would need to pull it straight up, like the lid of a garbage can. Clearly this had something to do with mental development. Mine as well as hers.

In the first place, it took me thirty minutes to take the thing out of its plastic packaging. Loading it with various kinds of bird treats—almonds, fruit berries, pellets, dried fruits, and peanuts in the shell—and putting it back together again took another twenty. Good luck, Lady.

If looking at treats she couldn't get didn't make her happy, it would certainly keep her occupied long enough for us to get some work done. This one, at least, was worth both the time it took to load it and the money it took to pay for it.

I fastened it up inside her cage and stepped back to enjoy a sense of accomplishment. Before I could even sit down to watch, Lady clambered off the perch from which she had been surveying me all this time and darted down the bars toward the toy.

Then she simply sat there riveted for a moment, examining the new foraging box closely. "Stumped," I thought. "Good."

In about a minute, she attacked the problem square on.

She opened the swing-away lid on the first box and the almonds disappeared.

She pulled up the lid on the second box and the dried fruit went.

She nudged open the window-like lid on the third box and downed the fruit berries in gulps.

And then, she simply pried open the swing-away top on the peanuts and sat, goober in claw, licking the thing like an ice-cream cone. She cracked the hull slowly and deliberately, a look of triumph in her eyes. To make her point, like a child bored by arithmetic problems, she moved away from the foraging box and never touched it again.

The project must have taken her all of about ten minutes.

Then she dropped down to the floor of her cage, lay on her back, feet straight up—the strangest bird trick you will ever see—and began to roll an empty toilet paper roll with her feet. Up and down the cage, over and under the perches, in and out of the tube for at least another twenty minutes. A toilet paper roll, her really favorite toy, occupied her for the rest of the afternoon.

Then she dashed out to the end of her drop-down door, jumped from the bars of it to the front of my sweater, looked me straight in the eye and waited for the real treat, the one she gets for being good. As in, "I opened all your silly toys, didn't I? Well, it's payback time."

So much for foraging.

Who won that day? Lady, of course. Lady and her toilet paper roll beats the big toys every single day.

———

There is something soporific about living in a culture of things. Our minds dull at the thought of them. In an attempt to "keep up," or "stay in the loop," or be part of the "race to the top," we find ourselves buried in a living coffin of things.

We begin to develop shelves full of the CDs and dishes and playthings we don't use anymore. They're out of date now. Too old to use anymore. "The lifetime of a computer," I heard a clerk say, "is at most three years now."

The problem in a technological society is not that a thing wears out as it did in an industrial society. It simply ceases to be usable, because the software now takes more memory than last year's computer had to spare. Or the cables have changed on the new one, which means that all of its peripherals have changed, too. It's not a matter now of buying a new computer—it's a matter of having to buy everything that goes with the computer, too: its external backup drive, the portable DVD that goes with it, the headphones it takes to listen to its videos. Not to mention the cover for it, a bag to carry everything in, the software to make it usable. The problem is that nothing is an item anymore; everything is a system.

And so we buy one system this year and find ourselves needing to buy an entirely new system three years from now.

There is no catching up. There is definitely no getting ahead of it all.

We live in a Disneyland of things. Inside of us, our souls bear the burden of watching what is fashionable today become useless tomorrow. We go through life paying for this year's models while last year's version of the same thing gathers dust in our closets. Like the great abandoned ziggurat temples of our ancient past, the things adored in earlier times have become this year's past idols.

Obsolescence has become our way of life.

What happens to our souls in the midst of a plague of materialism accounts in large part for how we think about our lives.

To live in a swamp of things dulls the soul. It becomes impossible to appreciate what we have anymore. It's always v1.0 in a v2.0 world. Always insufficient, in other words. Always inferior. Always behind the pack. The soul that develops that kind of perspective on the world can never completely relax in it. There is never enough of what we have to make our current life enough for us. The very virtue of gratitude, that fine-tuner of the happy mind, is smothered in the glut of things. Its voice muted, its soul gray.

Obsolescence makes us restless for what's coming next, rather than happy with the present. It's impossible to focus the mind on what I have—when all I can think about is what could be available soon. Life becomes an exercise in "if only." If only I had this; if only I could buy that; if only I could find the money for it—somehow.

The mantras of possibility become insatiable prods to design our lives around shopping rather than around living. We spend life trying to keep up with tomorrow, rather than on the sheer joy of living life today. We become attached to the peripherals of life and lose the taste of its juice. It's all about finding something new, something beyond what we have so far. We go through life keeping one eye on store windows rather than both eyes on the quality of what we already have.

Advertising drowns us in a plethora of claims about which choices—of all the unnecessary choices around us—are really right for us now. Nothing is sure anymore. "I could buy the leather living room suite or I could buy the vinyl one. The leather is more beautiful; the vinyl one will not spot. My best friend got the leather one . . ." Decision-making becomes more about what is on offer than about what I need. Or what is best for me now. Or what I can afford without taking essentials away from someone. It is a wrestling match of the soul, full of agitation, deprived of peace.

We find ourselves feeling forever unfinished, always incomplete. What is out there waiting for us yet becomes our measure of dissatisfaction with what we have. It makes envy a substitute for healthy ambition.

Indeed, we are in a strange moment in history. For the first time in human experience, for many of us, what we do not need is within our reach at all times, luring us, leading us beyond the goods of the soul. For all our so-called time-savers, we find ourselves with little time left now to pursue the things that bring peace and appreciation for life.

And what is the resolution of such a state of soul? Only this: we must learn to separate what brings us a taste of the depths of life from having things that keep us from enjoying life itself.

It's a choice between owning lots of toys and doing lots of foraging that we don't really need, and seeking instead the moments in life that last. It's about learning what gives us joy and fills our lives with a sense of relaxation and wonder, beauty and satisfaction. It's about sucking the sweetness out of being alive. Just being alive. For its own sake.

LADY THE PERFORMER

Play

Remember that I had two other birds before Lady. They were quiet little things, relatively sedentary, certainly self-contained. Bennie was more assertive than Billy, but not much. As long as she was in the same room with me, sitting on my shoulder, preferably, she wallowed in the bliss of it.

If her luck held and the top drawer of my desk was open, she could spend the entire afternoon mining it. One piece at a time, she picked each little gimcrack that had accumulated there over the years. She rolled it around on her tongue for awhile and then dropped it on the floor. Her joy was now complete.

Point: both of those birds were simply happy to sit and wait. Forever, if necessary. For who knows what.

Not Lady. Lady doesn't wait for anything to happen. Lady

makes things happen all by herself. She's what we would call "an effective woman"—if, indeed, she were a woman.

Nothing is foreign to Lady. She isn't afraid of anything. This bird is fearless, sassy, creative, and a perpetual play baby. The books say that you need to rotate their toys regularly, because parrots tire of them easily. Not this parrot. She has her favorites—the swing, the rope bridge, the chain with the bell on the end of it, the toilet paper roll. Don't even think of changing them.

Best of all, she's like an athlete in training. Whatever she does with each toy, she does over and over every day, just waiting for an audience to appear. By this time, she has clearly figured out when that is most likely. Breakfast on a Saturday is a good time. Anytime in the office seems possible. Afternoon in the garden room while people relax before supper usually works. Never mind. It doesn't really matter to Lady. She'll perform at any time. What matters is that people are there and people watch the show.

This, after all, is not just any old idle play period. This is an exercise in "Cirque du Soleil." This is a show for the judges, for the Bird Olympics. Up and over the cage top for the opening bow. Emcee, please call the audience to order. And then, the roar of the crowd: "Oh, oh, hereeeeesheeeegoesss!" So much for a quiet cup of hot coffee on a cold winter morning. Forget the light talk, you'll never be able to hear yourself. Never mind the television news. The Big Top is up; the show has begun.

There's a dash down the outside of the cage, a hop to the door ramp, a pause at the door for dramatic effect. Then, like any aerialist, the long, slow, high climb to the top of the dome and another hop to the swing.

Apparently she knows that parrots on swings give the whole thing a dash of Broadway. Lady stretches sinuously, one long bright wing at a time, just enough for all the gold edges to catch the light. Then she moves to the other leg and does it again. You can't help but wonder for a moment whether she's going to primp her head feathers, too.

Finally, she pumps up the swing a few times and grabs at the chain and baubles as she goes by. The show is on. She lets go of the swing, hangs on the chain by her beak, pulls herself straight up to the swing again, and, almost frenzied now, races back and forth from the chain to the perch to the swing to the spin at the end of the chain.

It's a display of great daring and total abandonment. All the bells on the cage ring as she shakes the unit from one end to another, five ounces of fury and fame let loose on the universe.

As her encore, she slips off the edge of the wire ramp in front of her cage door and throws herself upside down, standing now on her head, held up by only one claw. It's not perfect, of course. She has yet to really stand on her head—but if she knows that, she's not admitting it. After all, it is a headstand and—since we don't know any other bird that does one—it does not seem right to deny her the acclaim.

She ends the show as suddenly as she began and sits there on her porch solemnly, waiting for the applause, the huzzahs, the throwing of the bouquets—and, of course, the treat.

Then she steps daintily off the ramp in front of the cage and comes to the end of her Plexiglas porch, stretching toward the table where the bread and honey jar stay. This is not a show without a contract. This is not a performer without a sense of perfection. This is our very own Lady Hildegard, and we are her adoring public.

But most of all, she has much to teach us about what it means to be talented. What does she get out of all of this? Exactly what we do in our own moments of spotlight and approval: she gets to play for the attention and encouragement she gets. Proof that her existence has been noted, in a cosmos in which we are reminded that not even a sparrow falls to the ground unnoted.

It is a stunning display of talent and effort and self-worth from a creature most of the world hardly notices as they walk by.

The problem with play is that very few people take it seriously enough. Play, child psychologists insist, is essential to child-hood development. More than that, researchers in the effects of play make clear that play is important to our development as adults, as well. Which means, of course, that what we don't learn about play as children will certainly return to haunt us as we get older. It is the training ground, researchers affirm repeatedly, of both the happy child and the healthy adult.

The effects of play follow us through the years, always stretching us, often relaxing us, forever helping us test ourselves and eventually to reshape our worlds. It is the only arena in life where failure can be fun and creativity is really encouraged and talent can be tested without personal cost. It breaks the monotony of the well-ordered life and sends us back to face it, renewed and revived enough to dare to live it differently.

Most of all, perhaps, play releases the soul to see life differently than the rules say it must be. Playing with drums allows a legitimate sense of abandon. Running on the beach, cycling through a park, shooting hoops into a clothes basket on top of a ladder release a new kind of vitality in us.

Most of all, play teaches a child that there are different ways to do things than the world says they must be done. We can bang to our heart's content. We can run through the water rather than on the sand. We can get off the bike to smell flowers. We can play basketball for candies rather than points. We can, in other words, make up an entirely new world for ourself, one in which we're in charge of the way things go, one where winning is not what life is about.

Then someday we finally come to realize that all of life is a game, really, and some of its rules simply don't work anymore. In fact, some of the rules actually make the game impossible to play. A few of them take the fun out of life entirely.

We learn that, yes, we can change the rules that guide our own lives, too. No matter who says otherwise, we don't really have to go to college. If starting our own itinerant repair business feels like more fun to us than computer science or accounting, we can make up our education game as we go.

We learn from play both the costs and benefits of risk, of stepping outside the lines of life to see what might be on the other side of them. The risks we take will win us some and lose us some, of course. But, having won once or twice along the way—when trying was its own reward—we know that risk is not always wrong. We learn from play that risk can be the beginning of other ways to become our best at the game of life.

Most of all, perhaps, we learn in play to be flexible, to realize that losing does not mean that we will never play again. It means that we must learn how to lose and then return to play again. Lose better. Learn better. Play again. Until it becomes the mantra of the healthy adult life.

The nice thing about play is that it can be done either alone or with the other. In either case, ironically, it teaches us something about communication, about bringing to the world in other forms what we have learned through experimenting with our own talents. Having learned to lose, whether playing on a team or shooting hoops alone in the backyard, we know clearly that there is no such thing as always winning. We learn, too, that there are other people with other scores, all of them better than ours, at least in some places in life. And so we are prepared not only to lose but to respect those with talents beyond our own.

It makes us capable of playing the game of life with people who excel in things in which we do not. We learn that they deserve the accolades they get and that their talents are not a threat, they are simply different than our own. And with that insight alone, learned at least subconsciously as a child at play, we become better, more pleasant, more appreciative, more trusting members of humankind.

In today's world, in particular, play holds a special place. It is also in today's world that the lack of play has a particular effect on society in general. The rewards of play are many:

Play is as therapeutic as it is socially or physically developmental.

Play keeps society sane in a world where time never ends. Before the invention of the lightbulb, the day ended when daylight ended. There was little or nothing that could be done from the beginning of dark to the breaking of dawn. Sleep, rest, relaxation were built right into the human clock.

But not now. Now we live in a war against rest, a world without pause buttons, at a time when the pressure—immediate, local, global, personal—has never been higher.

Society without play is society—you and I—on a very short fuse. Living on a human treadmill—a two-hour commute every day, forty to fifty hours of work every week—life is an endless cycle of work without rest. Add to that four or five hours a day trying to catch up with the basics of life like shopping, cooking, fixing, cleaning, family, there's little time left for living. We find ourselves with nothing but sleep time to get us ready to do our best work the next day. And what happens to the blooming of the human soul then?

That kind of living is dangerous. It is dangerous for the person whose nerves are frayed to the root. It's a dangerous time for the companies that count on their concentration or their creativity. It is dangerous time for us all, for the person, for their work, for the world they hope to shape. It is a life fraught with tension, the kind that endangers marriages and mental health, family and full human development.

And only by learning to play can we even begin to heal such an overwrought world, our own overwrought souls.

The question we are required to ask is how much play is there in our world? The happiness of our lives may well depend on the answer.

LADY SHOWS EMOTION

———

Love

Lady collects people. She knows how to woo them, how to lure them, how to manipulate them. She gets what she wants with a chirp and a kiss and a winsome look that would melt the ice off of Mount Olympus.

If Lady has been clear about anything since she came, it is that she bonds easily with people and is not sitting in wait to attack them. She cuddles. She snuggles. She pinches. And she picks at skin tags and moles every chance she gets. Sometimes even at earlobes. But serious or random biting is not her usual response to anything.

In fact, Lady, like most caiques, loves to be handled. She will lie on her back in your hand and look up at you with the most languorous of eyes. Asleep in a cradle of love.

Or she will stand on your chest and raise her wings to get her undersides scratched.

She waits to have the back of her neck scratched and will twist and turn her head this way and that till you get it right. It's a game of "here" and "no, not there," as much loved for the game of it as for the scratch itself, I think.

She does a trick of twist and turn through your fingers till you tire long before she does.

On the other hand, always on watch for hawks, she is forever loath to allow anyone to put a hand over her head. She does discriminate, in other words. She just doesn't allow her fears to control her. Usually. But there have been times.

If animals expose to us, unmasked and unambiguous, our own raw emotions, then two incidents with Lady stand out with such stark clarity that it's impossible for them not to give us pause. In the first instance, Lady met a friend but didn't know it. In the second, Lady met a stranger.

On this day, one of Lady's new friends, a gentle woman with a loving voice, stopped in the office to say goodnight. She was new to the staff but, unlike most of us, had come with a bit of experience with birds herself. She took to Lady immediately and, apparently, Lady to her. There were treats and sweet words and long talks between them. Lady was getting the attention she loves most. No problem here.

But this day, with the wind lashing outside the windows and the snow falling for the third day in a row, Anne, the new friend, came to the cage dressed in a great black coat and furry collar. Her head was almost lost in the cavern of the hood that came with it. The voice was just as sweet, though, and the treat was a good one. She rushed over to the cage to get their good-bye in before the car came to the door.

Just inches away from Lady's face, the woman leaned into the top of the cage and brought her hand up, fingers out, for Lady to climb on one last time for the day. It was the most natural gesture in Lady's life. Person after person picks her up countless times a day. And Lady loves it. Nothing says "treat" or "walk" or "adventure" or "play" more clearly than do two fingers outstretched. The opportunity has almost never been refused. At least until then. Until that particular moment.

Lady gripped the wires of her cage top and waited. Her feathers were slicked down, her wings taut and ready against her body. Her new friend talked to her again. "Good night, Lady. Be a good bird till I see you tomorrow . . ." And then, without warning, for no apparent reason, suddenly, Lady reached out and snapped. Everybody in the office saw the blood.

Was it the big black coat? The high, deep hood? The face hidden in swirls of wool? Who will ever know?

Lady is taken to the office every day down a hallway of toddler and preschool activities. "Bird lady, bird lady," the children begin to squeal at the sight of her. Clinging to the coat collar of her carrier, Lady bounces along, oblivious of the tiny hands stretching up to touch her. Children, the books say, ought not to be allowed too close to parrots for fear the bird becomes agitated by the motions. In this case, other than her walk down the hall, Lady lives in a totally adult environment. No worry there.

So, when Brigid, the six-year-old friend of a staffer, asks to visit Lady, I'm on full alert. One quick motion, one loud noise, could start something that in the end would upset both the bird and the child.

Brigid is a gentle and sensitive child, not given to quick actions or loud squealing, but totally in love with animals. And Lady Hildegard fascinates her. If you are six years old, after all, how many birds are there in your life who will let you touch their feet or listen as you talk to them? Best of all, Brigid moves slowly and quietly. No worry here about frightening the bird with the moving sleeves of a big black coat or a large hood.

Nevertheless, it pays to be cautious. Brigid is a child—and a stranger. I am prepared for the visit. But the little girl, true to form, comes almost tiptoeing around the frame of the office door.

Brigid's a normally hesitant child, but, for some reason, not with Lady. Instead, she walked straight to the edge of the cage and simply stood there. Most surprising of all, Lady, too, came to the end of her little porch and, just as quietly and simply as Brigid had done, stood there waiting. I could see them look hard and long into one another's eyes, neither of them blinking, both of them solemn and steady as Doric columns, not a word said.

It was a mystical moment. The bird and the child were locked in some kind of preternatural connection. Lady moved slowly and sweetly to Brigid's fingers, and Brigid leaned over and smiled a smile as fragile as the dew. The sense of satisfied love and shy spiritual awe on her small face lit up the entire room.

In moments like that it's suddenly clear what was really meant to happen at the naming of the animals. And yet, as the first instance showed, not all encounters between human caretakers and our animal companions are so soft.

But one thing was clear in both cases: Love and fear, fear and love are motivators that lie very close to the surface in all of us. Animals we call "irrational." Ourselves we tout as the acme of creation. We rationalize. We give ourselves reasons for being irrational. But in the end, it's all the same, isn't it? We each do things we either can't explain or can't justify. And so we spend our entire lives explaining and justifying—and we never even have the grace to blush.

———

Life is a struggle between caution and courage, between reck-lessness and prudence, between bright spirits and common sense. At least that's the message that most of us get growing up. You must always "be careful." And at the same time, you must "have faith" that all things will be right in the end.

It is life lived on a breathless edge—between the foolhardi-ness of love and the fringes of fear. It is equivalent to being in a place where anything can happen, including the worst.

When we react out of love, life is full of the impossible and the good. All for us. So what can ever stop us now?

When fear controls us, life is lived carefully, watching every step, because, after all, the worst can happen at any moment.

It is a frightening way to go through life, fearful that love may not last or that failure may finally defeat us in the end. But surely it doesn't have to be that way. Surely we do not need to surrender our ability to bring love where love is not, and instead simply wait for love to come to us. And surely we are not meant to be casualties of our own reluctance to forgo fear in favor of fidelity to the fundamental goodness of life.

Instead, there are ways to both bolster the love quotient that sets us free and damp the fear factor that nails our feet to the floor. We can learn, if we want, to approach life with arms open and heads up. We can refuse to give in to a view of life that is dangerous and defeating before it even begins. We can learn to be open without being reckless.

We can distinguish the kind of fear that is sensible and salvific from the kind of fear that is neurotic and paralyzing.

Fear is the enemy of the soul that limits our ability to love life as it is. Fear divides life into categories of safe and unsafe, good and bad, acceptable and unacceptable. And so we stand where we are, frozen to the spot, certain that being safe is better than being free.

The person for whom fear is the demon in the dark must forever require themselves to go one step further than their spiritual strength seems to allow. They must let go and trust that the Spirit who inspires us to move on will take us there.

To allow fear to control us means that we will never be able to do anything beyond the mundane, the familiar, the regular, the safe. It undermines self-confidence and allows us to believe our own worst nightmares. We are closed off from the unknown where real living lies and where the self becomes more than even we ourselves could ever imagine.

When fear consumes us, we have no time for anything else. We have no vision of how to construct for ourselves a world of lights and stars, of hope and possibility, of life and liveliness.

Only love can do those things for us.

But to allow love to lead us, we must be willing to be led into the unknown with arms open. There must be no one who is excluded from the embrace. There must be nothing called "foreign" in our hearts.

Love enables us because it numbs us to fear. It is the one bridge we have to connect us to the unknown other. It's love that leads us into unknown places and opens undeveloped possibilities within us. It generates new life both within us and around us. It is the only real proof we have that we can, without doubt, come to fullness of life. Having experienced the security, the safety, and the certainty of love, all of life becomes secure. Having known love once, we have what it takes to make it happen for others and so to increase our own.

Once we put down fear and open our lives to love, then fear cannot trigger in us the need to defend ourselves from what has never hurt us.

Once we have allowed ourselves to love first—because we ourselves have first been loved by someone else—all of life takes on the color of care and the certainty of comfort. It creates the confidence that comes from knowing that, however uncertain tomorrow may be, we will not be in it alone. That, if nothing else, will keep our hearts open and our souls attuned to the presence of goodness in the unknown, the uncharted, the undiscovered, and the unexplored.

LADY ON THE MOVE

Adventure

Every bird owner has a decision to make: Shall this bird have her wings clipped or shall she be flighted? It's not an easy decision. A flighted bird in a room with a ceiling fan is in grave danger. A flighted bird can land on hot stovetops or in swirling toilet bowls. They can slip out slow-closing screen doors in minutes.

So that's why Lady's wings are clipped. She has done all of it, including the toilet bowl.

The temptation is to feel sorry for the bird who cannot fly—who lives rooted in place, totally cut off from the rest of civilization, denied her natural mobility. Scandalous.

Well, not here. Flight wings or no flight wings, Lady is a traveler. Call it compensation or call it intelligence, whatever it is, it works for Lady. Lady's life is a veritable milk run: she gets up in the morning, goes downstairs for breakfast, slips under someone's coat to get taken to work, and goes from one office to the other to see all her friends during the day.

In between times, she catches a ride from anyone and everyone who comes within two feet of the cage. If you have your arms down when you get within distance, she grabs a cuff. If you bend over to get something off the table beside the cage, she hooks her beak into the end of your jacket. If you reach down to give her a treat, she jumps on your shoulder. And if you say, "Lady, wanna take me for a walk?" she jumps on your finger, turns her back to you and plays ship's captain, or car driver, or plane pilot. Whatever it is, she doesn't seem to get the relationship between your finger and your body, and then she keeps turning around to make sure you're following her.

Trust me, this is a bird on the move.

Her favorite sound is the tinkle of car keys. "Wanna go, Lady? Wanna go?" is enough to set the cage ablaze. The very thought of a ride in the car can start her quivering with excitement. She stretches herself out to her full length, bobs until the cage shakes, and then starts the chatter that announces her coming presence to the rest of the world. Now it's either take her or put up with the cries of agony that come from the abandoned and disconsolate.

The first time we took her out in the car, when we came out of the store, we found it surrounded by people. Lady was sitting on the dashboard, holding court with old ladies and small children, the center of adoring attention, her favorite place in life. Another time, a lady wanted to buy her. And a third time, she begged till she was allowed out of the car to sit beside us at our outside table to have her own bite of bagel for lunch. The fact that everybody in the food court stared at us all through the entire meal didn't bother Lady at all.

The car is well-equipped by now. We have a blanket, a potty perch, a toy or two, and a plastic platform stuck to the window on the passenger side of the car. She sits there chattering at all the cars that go by or following the flight of birds overhead.

She gets incensed at the sight of large 18-wheelers that cut off her view of the fields and woods on the other side of the road.

When she tires of the passing parade she crawls onto the driver's neck, buries herself in her hair, and goes sound asleep till the car pulls in to the next toll booth.

Then, the fun begins. She frightened one woman attendant in a booth by trying to take the toll ticket and steal the money before the officer could reach out to get it herself.

In fact, Lady is quite accustomed to picking me up at strange airports and sharing my supper all the way home.

Whatever it is, wherever we go, Lady is contented. The operational word is "go." There are no ruts in Lady's life, no places so dull that she can't amuse herself in them, no moments not worth living.

She's always active. She never stops moving. She wastes not a minute of life. If anything, she seems starved for more and more and more of it. I have learned a great deal from Lady. In fact, she teaches us all to expect the unexpected in life.

If Lady has anything to say about life at all, it's got to be that we need to be cautious when we see something that we've never seen before. We need to remember that what we're seeing is not necessarily wrong. It is simply another way of going through life which, if we watch carefully, may teach us to do our own life differently, and better, too.

One thing we know how to do in the developed world is to buy excitement. We go to places other people tell us are exotic. We eat in expensive restaurants and so think we have come to understand food. We vacation in resorts that package our fun for us and schedule our activities. We join great crowds of tourists and all do the same things together and think we have discovered the unique experience of what it means to be alive.

In today's society, we make everything a business and, recently, leisure most of all.

We are paying people to tell us how to have an adventure. The notion of simply walking into the woods to see for ourselves what's there is an old-fashioned one now. The thought of just choosing a city and doing a walking tour of our favorite kinds of places—let alone of the places we know least about—is unheard of. The definition of an adventure now is to go as far away from where we are as we can and let someone else tell us how to enjoy it.

In the West we have event planners and tour guides and travel agents to pick our shows and buy our tickets and choose our seats and order our dinners.

So sophisticated are we in the fine art of being told where to go and what to do, most people don't know their own cities. They'll take a tour to another city rather than venture out of their comfort zone to see what's already there in the city in which they live.

So, in the end, we do "tours," not adventures. Tours happen when someone else picks us up and takes us where they tell us everybody should go. As a result, even our leisure, even what is meant to be the unstructured hours of life, comes digested by someone else before we get to it. They are trips advertised like dressing gowns as "one size fits all."

But adventures are something else entirely.

Adventures happen when we ask questions, like who exactly was Oliver Hazard Perry?—a hero of the War of 1812, whose statue we pass daily in the park—and then find the answers to them ourselves. Adventures affect our very lives. They change our idea of what it means to live in a place, to know the place, to learn from the place. They force us to explore the obvious and find there, in the hidden recesses of our own life, the mystery tour of our own lives.

It is those things we remember when all the standard-brand travel is over.

We remember walking down the creek till we found the only trout hole in the area. We can't forget the day in the backyard when we learned to target shoot using old cans and bottles. We can see in our mind's eye forever the days we spent barbecuing hamburgers by the lake while we collected all the different wild flowers we could find.

Adventures happen when we take the time to do what we have not done before. Then we discover what has lain within the borders of our own lives, but which we have never bothered to explore. It is an excursion intent on learning more about the obvious, like tracing the history of all the pictures that hang in our own house.

It is this spirit of adventure within us that determines the excitement level of our own lives. But it does not start with an activity itself. It starts with the taste for adventure that has been nurtured within us. And it relies on curiosity and commitment.

Only curiosity can lead us where we have never been. It is the insatiable desire to know what it is not necessary to know—but which, once discovered, changes the very way we look at the rest of life.

It is the willingness to stray outside the ruts in the road, to go where we have not been before. It is the spiritual discipline of talking to people we would never meet otherwise. It is the fun of eating foods we have never tasted till now, of mixing with strangers and making them friends. It is the process of defeating our fear of the unknown and making it a part of our own lives. An adventure is an excursion beyond the fringes of life as we have ever known it. It commits us to going to the end of every interest, of every question mark in our minds.

And why do it? Because it fills in the gaps in our own background and experience. It makes us bigger than we would otherwise be. It lifts us out of the humdrum of our own lives and gives us new energy and fresh joy.

Adventures come in a variety of ways. There is no one form only. Many of them are physical, of course. They take us to unknown places or into great physical feats. We rock climb. Or travel to the Arctic Circle. Or compete for a place in *The Guinness Book of Records*.

But there are other kinds of adventures that stretch the soul more than the body. In the end, that kind of adventure can do as much to change our view of life as a climb up Mount Everest might do for someone else. Making my own first movie, or boating down the Atlantic Intracoastal Waterway, or painting my own first picture, bring out an entirely new part of us. Every adventure we undertake leaves us with more soul, more heart, than we ever had before.

Exploring where we have never been before, doing what we have never done before—doing things that are seldom done by anyone—constitutes an adventure of the soul.

Like flighted birds with clipped wings, we must refuse to allow clipped wings to hold us back. No, we cannot do everything in life—but we can do what we have never done before. We can become something we never thought we were. We can take personal responsibility for becoming alive intellectually, for experiencing the world rather than simply reading about it. We can challenge ourselves, push ourselves to the fullness of our physical powers, in order to discover what being human is really all about.

Then we may discover that life itself is the adventure that it is meant to be. Only when we ourselves test every boundary, explore every question, reach for every experience within our grasp, can we possibly hope to spark the fire in our souls that will light our way through those rare moments in life that are dark and dull.

Then we, too, can let our souls fly free, whether we can fly or not. Then we shall have refused to allow limitations to become the definition of what we mean when we say to ourselves, Am I alive—or not?

LADY'S ASPIRATIONS

Essence

There was a time when our office was the standard brand, normal type: two computer desks, a wall of metal file cabinets, a work table, a few chairs. This was definitely the no-nonsense kind of place that people like to think is "productive" because it is stripped down, purely functional, Spartan. There was not an unnecessary piece of equipment in sight, not so much as an extra mail opener.

We came to work every day, went straight to our desks and began the steady, silent list of normal office routines. Go through emails, pass on the messages, start the file work, do the callbacks. Nice, regular, orderly. The dull, steady kind of work that people without animal companions can take for granted.

But that was before the birds came: Bennie first, an almost invisible addendum to the scene; now Lady, reigning over the territory from the throne in her head, vociferously, imperiously, unpredictably.

Now the office is her throne room, a scene reminiscent of Hollywood's *The Last Emperor*. There the child-sovereign sits enthroned on a minuscule dais surrounded by emptiness. In this case, the throne is a small cage atop a rolling table, with a supply shelf underneath.

Even that setup seemed relatively normal at the beginning. Until Lady figured out how to walk upside down under the table top. Pulling her light little body along the brace of it with her beak, she gets into position over the treat jars. And now, hanging upside down, she pops the lids off the jars and binges on the treat of the day.

Of all the things I have learned from Lady, one of them is this: there is no way to birdproof a room. Birds walk and waddle easily over obstacles; they climb and glide from one chair to another; they jump from surface to surface. In cases of extreme curiosity, they simply throw themselves onto the floor from the top of the cage, get up, shake themselves off, and start the excursion from there.

Every room is Disneyland to Lady, new games to play there, a new funland to explore. You get accustomed to finding birds under things and you learn quickly to pick them up and put them back on the cage again. Where they will stay—until the next thing catches their eye.

In this case, who could have thought what it could possibly be?

Lady's rolling table sits parallel to the bank of metal file cabinets that line one whole wall of the office. If you're working at the computer from either desk, you wouldn't even see her. And nobody did.

Those files took hours, days, months—some of them even a couple years—to organize, categorize, label. The labels are particularly important, because you could not even begin to leaf idly through hundreds of folders gathered over the years to look for a subhead of a subhead of a major category.

Lady enjoys a romp on the floor every once in a while—but it's "up" that fascinates her. Whatever the highest point in the room, she heads for it every time.

There are some things birds can do, but, nevertheless, a lot of things they cannot. Climbing file cabinets is one of them. We were sure of that.

Being certain you know what a bird can't do is why being perpetually wrong can get to be so common for bird owners. It's good for the humility; it's not so great for sanity.

In this case, no one in the office heard a thing. In fact, it was so quiet in the room that day, people simply forgot Lady was even there. Until someone heard the clawing and looked up.

There she hung. Flat against the file cabinet, her little claws reaching and slipping and reaching and slipping on the metal, again and again. She was halfway up and halfway down. With nowhere to go and no way to get there. No way whatsoever to launch a jump back to the top of the cage.

The metal file drawers are standard but smooth. At the bottom of each drawer there's a screw. There's a handle above the screw. And above the handle is a label holder. Think of it if you're a bird with a height fetish: all you need to do is to stretch yourself out till you can grab the screw. Then, using it for balance, swing over to the drawer and stand on the screw till you can climb onto the handle. From there pull yourself up on the label holder and then, hanging for dear life on its thin edges, reach up again and get a hold of the next screw. And then start all over again—grab the screw, climb onto the handle, get a hold of the label holder. Easy. It may take a little time to negotiate each drawer, but the effort is worth it. There's a live plant on the top of the file cabinet, yes, but there's even more fun than that on the way to the top.

The proof of the real fun was clear: every label on every drawer had already been taken out of its holder, chewed to pieces, and dropped on the floor, where "Catholic Church–Religious Life" now read " . . . olic Church–Relig . . ." The glint in Lady's eye was beautiful to behold.

It isn't what Lady does that presents either a challenge or a life lesson. It's what she will do next that haunts a person. It is her insatiable appetite for whatever life has on offer for the next time that gives a person pause. Where does it come from? How do you handle it? Should you handle it?

There is in Lady a voracious appetite for becoming: nothing in life is good enough for her just because it's there and handy and possible. It's what she might do that she has never done before, that gives her that extra dash of life to challenge your own.

I worry that some day she will overdo herself and get caught or hurt on something. But if and when that is the case, we will have one consolation. We will know, as do the families of children who insist on mountain climbing, that they were never happier than when they were doing more of the same.

Lady's life lesson is about drinking life to the dregs, about always striving to get to the top of it, to the essence of it, to the marrow of it. And whatever the situation, to keep on trying to the end.

In a world of things, life can be so easily drowned in superficialities. We are surrounded by accoutrements of life that we have come to think are of its essence. We think that computers are work and big houses are success and plastic flowers are beauty. And so, we get further away by the day from the heartbeat of life.

The marrow of life, like marrow is in the human body, is what gives us spirit and zest and zing. It's what makes all the rest of it—the work, the people, the structure, the projects, the programs—worthwhile. It has something to do with the very meaning of life—both the meaning we give it and the meaning we see in it.

To measure the marrow of our own lives, we must be about the business of answering the question, What is life all about and for what am I myself here?

If life is only about work, what happens to us—to life—when the work ends?

If life is only about people, what is left for us when they go?

If life is about the rules we keep, what does it mean to break them, as we all do, sometime, somehow?

If being part of a system is what gives life value, and that system fails, what does that say about the value of my own life?

If life is about being part of somebody's project, what's my life worth when that project ends and no one invites me to be part of the next one?

To peel back life to its essence, to its marrow, is to strip away everything that purports to substitute for life until I am actually left with myself alone. And now what is life about? Surely the answer is clear: life is really only about what I believe that I am meant to do to make it better. For myself, of course, but for others, as well.

It means knowing the prize and then concentrating on it, whatever the obstacles to reaching it, however long the journey it will take to get there. It is about having a goal in life that is big enough to be worth spending your life to achieve. Whether it is ever achieved or not. As the Sufi master said, "If you expect to find an answer to your question, you have simply not asked a big enough question."

Maybe saving the planet is a goal that touches the very center of your soul. Maybe your resonance with nature is so strong that the very thought of dried-up rivers and lost species and shriveling forests pains your soul. Then the marrow of life for you is to embrace that identity. Make it count. Align yourself with other people who believe that passing creation on to the next generation alive and whole is the reason they are alive.

Maybe the realization that there is a new slavery on the planet raises the temperature of your soul to white heat. Maybe you have come to realize, but not fully admit, that this underground slavery deals in small girls and powerless women and sells them from over one border to another. Maybe the very thought of forcing women to do unpaid corporate work for billionaire corporations or to perform the loveless sex services that the powerful demand breaks your heart. Then, perhaps, to save the marrow of your own soul, you become an outspoken advocate for national sanctions against this plague on the planet.

Maybe you travel to one of the hovels of the world, smell the stink of its poverty, see the wounds of starvation in toothless adults and lethargic children there. Then, safe at home again, dedicate some given percentage of your own salary to support the aid workers who are giving their very lives to save them.

It is those things in us—consciousness, support, and commitment—that take us into the very marrow of life. It makes us part of the lifeblood of the planet. It makes us fully human, human beings. It brings us to the point where we become part of creation, rather than merely observers of it.

We become the guards on the ramparts of life. We become the trumpeters who call the attention of the powerful to where their power is needed. We become the voice of creation crying out for the sake of all the world.

The marrow of life is not found and not lived on the surface of life. It resides in the soul of the planet where our own heart beats with it as one.

Then we find ourselves going where we would least expect to be, reaching higher for the stars, reaching deeper into ourselves for the real reason we are here. If we have any marrow in us at all, we know we must decide what we ourselves are meant to do about it. Then, no effort is too much, no climb is too difficult, no goal is too high.

LADY STEPS UP

Respect

Lady's quite capable of using human speech. After I put the cover over her cage at night, I can hear her practicing syllables in the dark quite regularly, in fact. She presses her beak into the corner of the bars and goes on and on, all to herself. But practice or no practice, she's not inclined to say much. And why would she? She can get everything she wants without the effort of having to practice a foreign language to ask for it.

What's more, what she really likes best is pure, unadulterated chatter and whistles. Sound for its own sake. Certainly not for ours. She will sit on the top of her cage making strange bits of garble for hours. Sometimes she paces back and forth, going from one side of the cage to the other giving out screeches, or scoldings, first in one key, then in another. If you listen long enough, you'd swear she's reading from a script and taking parts.

But as far as nice, quiet, conversant human speech goes? Seldom and little. And then only with a sense of real intent. "Pretty baby" when she's trying to charm someone. "Arrrr-reeeen!" when she wants to go out the door with Maureen, one of her favorite people. Every once in a while she bellows, "No scream!"—a little snippet she picked up from me. Needless to say, I shouted it at her first and now she uses it on me when she's being defiant about other things.

Lady is not a robot. She doesn't do anything simply because she's been told to do it. It can take a lot of convincing to get her to want to do what you want her to do.

So, shortly after I'd had knee surgery, I was having enough trouble getting myself ready in the morning, without having to talk Lady into getting ready, too. "Joan," I heard Maureen say, "would you like me to take Lady downstairs for you?"

Don't tell me that the age of miracles is over. I couldn't have been more grateful.

The conversation I heard from across the room went something like this: "All right, Lady, let's go now. Get on your potty perch. That's a girl. Now," she said, stretching out the two fingers that signal Lady that it's time to go somewhere, "Now, step up. Come on now, Lady, step up. Lady, we have to go. Step up! Lady, we are going to be late for prayer. Step up—right now! Step up!"

I smiled to myself across the room. I couldn't wait to see who would win this one.

Every morning it was the same routine. Right down to the final exclamation point. As in, "Step up, Lady. Right now! Step up!"

It was at least a month later, maybe more. We were sitting

at the breakfast nook downstairs after prayer. Lady was on her cage, unusually quiet and obviously planning something. Then, suddenly, she stretched herself out, looked down the length of the breakfast table, and began to bob up and down, fast, faster, fastest. She was looking straight at Maureen.

"Lady," I said, "do you want to go see Maureen?" Lady jumped on my fingers. "Maureen," I said, leaning toward her with the bird, "do you want to take Lady?"

But before Maureen could get herself focused and her head completely out of the newspaper, Lady was already poised to go. She jumped on Maureen's sweater, looked up straight into her eyes, and yelled at the top of her deep gravelly voice, "Step up! Right now! Step up!" Intonation and all.

It was one of those "in-your-face" moments that bring us all to heart-stopping self-awareness, to a clear, direct sense of the way we sound to others. There was no confusing the message: "And how do you like being barked at?!" was loud and plain as Judgment Day.

After that, I noticed that the conversation between them changed to, "Wanna get up, Lady?" or "Are you ready to go, Lady?" or "Would you like a treat, Lady?" In a minute she had taught all of us to remember the civility we sometimes forget.

On the other hand, Lady also signaled a new order of things. Knowingly or not, she triggered a kind of emotional coup. "Step up, right now, step up" has become a rallying cry. Except that it's not from us to her anymore. It's from her to us. She clearly knows that "Step up" is an order. But she has clearly forgotten—or refuses to remember—that it was our order to her. Now she thinks that now it's her order to give to us.

So, if you're out of the room you hear, "Step up!" meaning,

"Come in here right now!" And if she wants you to give her something to eat, it's "Step up!" And if she wants a cuddle, it's "Step up," too.

Lady has made her point and it has been a clear one. There are simply some things that need to be done with more feeling than content. Lady, like us, it seems, was not born to take orders. She was born to create relationships. And people in a relationship speak softly to one another. They care as much about what the other person is feeling as they do about what they may or may not want.

It's been a strange turn of events. Like any young adult, Lady staked a claim that day, one that said, "I am a creature, too. Talk to me nicely." The lesson has been an overwhelming one, coming as it did from five ounces of feathers. It has reminded us that the world is filled with mind. Ours is not the only one. And all of us deserve the respect that comes with it. Because, as the scriptures say clearly: "God saw that it was good." All of it. Not some of it good and some of it—us—better.

When animals speak up to require respect and understanding and a little coaxing on the side, the human-animal scale balances a bit. We must thank them for that. They save us from the insufferable arrogance that comes with those who have been in the habit of defining their own superiority.

———

The modern world lives on rankings. It's the way we signal what we respect. In too many ways, it also signals what we say we don't need to respect at all.

As the dictionary puts it, "hierarchy is any system of persons or things ranked one above another." It's a tricky system because, though it organizes life nicely, it also categorizes it. The people or things on the top of the ladder loom ominously over the rest of it. It counts all of the rest of them lesser—less worthy of respect, less deserving of notice, less important to the world. Like vegetation over rocks, for instance. Or oil over air. Or humans over elephants, maybe.

Or, most ominous of all, it also categorizes within the large categories—like humans—as whites over blacks, priestly castes over untouchables, men over women, the wealthy over the poor.

As a result, ranking systems actually tell a very limited truth about the effect of ranking on the categories it purports to define.

The process of ranking things denies one dimension of importance in order to emphasize another one. For instance, a classic ecological court case—the 1973 case of the snail darter versus the Tellico Dam Project in Tennessee—left the world confused. It pitted one kind of importance against another at least as significant, if not an even more paramount understanding of the situation.

What was really more important, the Tellico Dam Project asked: water for human beings or the preservation of a small, unknown fish whose spawning grounds were in the area where the dam would be built?

In the hierarchy of animal-human considerations, the answer seemed obvious: water for humans, the top of the hierarchy, would be given priority. But if truth were known, there were multiple other places the dam could be built that would not threaten an endangered species, and so the food chain with it. Furthermore, the biodiversity of the ecological system would be saved and, therefore, eventually the well-being of humanity itself.

And yet we go on insisting on the superiority of one

dimension over another. We place a lot of stock in hierarchies and apply respect accordingly. The very fact of setting up a hierarchy implies that there is an answer to questions like, What is the best of all these things? Who is the most valuable here? But then, what is the value of everything else on the ladder? What will happen to the rest of us who are not on top of it? And what happens to respect in a system like this?

Indeed, hierarchies are downright dangerous. They argue for inequality by their very existence. In fact, they justify it.

We ranked creation—rocks, trees, water, and air—on the bottom, and people—males, really—on the top. The sorry effect of the ramifications of that kind of system made the elimination of the snail-darter fish of no concern whatsoever to dam builders and developers. What that decision will mean to generations of people after us remains to be seen.

In our own time, we have locked people into systems which, we argued, biology itself had unequivocally defined. When people on the top of the creation hierarchy named themselves the masters of the universe, their classifications of everything else determined their fate. And respect dissolved in a mist of power. Age after age after age.

Slaves were born to be slaves, we decided. Serfs were bound to the land—meaning, got bought and sold with it, non-whites were inferior, women were second-class human beings, and animals and everything else were for our use. No holds barred. No questions asked. No reasons given. Life was just one large cornucopia of good things for the people on top: churchmen and nobles, white men and warriors, the privileged and the powerful.

Clearly, hierarchy creates inequality and then calls it God's will.

But as hierarchy flourishes, so does intolerance and abuse. Until, eventually, the rest of the system learns to give up habitat and give up power and give up hope. Species die out, the quality of life gives way to air pollution and drought, and the social house of cards crumbles—one region, one group of people at a time.

Animals, most of all, suffer: They become our food and our biology experiments, our testing ground for cosmetics and our beasts of burden. They're left to starve when we're done with them, or hunted to death for the financial profit of their tusks or their skins, their furs or their antlers.

Just as sad—or even deadlier in terms of the effects of hierarchy on the human enterprise—is the fact that the assumptions of hierarchy separate what should be together. It makes humans the pinnacle of life and far above the concerns of those below them on life's pyramid. In the end, the two become distinctly different in the human mind and are treated likewise. One, the human, with deference; the other, the entire animal world, with disrespect.

The very powerful find little to be concerned and less to identify with where the life quality of the powerless is concerned. The notion of human respect for animal life fades into fantasy once the definitions of differences between the two mean more than what is alike about us: our common feelings and needs and contributions to life in general. The awareness that in many ways animal intelligence is far more developed than human reason escapes us. Then we allow ourselves to treat animals like things and not like living, breathing, thinking, feeling animals at all.

AFTERWORD

Danny, Duffy, and Lady—I have been in awe of their personalities, their intelligence, their feelings. In so many ways, they have exposed me to myself. They have softened the hardness out of me at the end of long and weary days. They have amused me and distracted me from myself. Most of all, I have learned a great deal from each of them.

I learned by watching them what no amount of theory, no degree of reading, no version of anybody's catechism could ever have taught me:

I learned to accept what I could not change in life, to live with it well, and to squeeze every ounce of juice out of what is.

I've discovered that self-knowledge is much more important in life than knowledge for its own sake. Only when we have suffered from our own limitations are we ready to really concentrate on being the best of whoever we are.

They taught me that enjoyment is a necessary part of life, the part that refreshes us and sends us on our way with a new burst of energy, free of heart. Pleasure, I came to realize because of them, is not a waste of time, not a lesser demonstration of what it means to be human.

Their assertiveness in the face of frustration and external control made me consider my own reactions to what I could not control.

I saw their sensitivities and began to give more thought to my own. I saw empathy become the bridge between us as separate species.

Being with them, I came to realize that each of us has a

special purpose and realized that the discovery of our own talents is key to our own purpose in life.

In each of them, it was what they could not do that endeared them to me as much as their special abilities. I came to see that none of us needs to do everything well. We just need to do something well because that is why we're here.

In their eyes, sad or confused, I could see the effects of rejection on us all and began to realize that learning to accept one another is what binds us all together. I saw that relationships are made as much of what we lack and need from one another, as they are because of what we have to offer and contribute.

I saw each of them develop in phases, a bit at a time. Life is a process, I could see, not an event. We grow at our own speed and there is no reason ever to despair that it will yet happen.

Clearly, the expectations that others have of us can do as much harm as they do good. It's finding our own gifts and interests and goals that really make the difference to the fullness of development in each of us.

In them all I saw varying degrees of excitement and play, of love and fear. I saw them court adventure and give themselves totally to life. I found in them companions that knew no end of devotion, no thought of rejection.

With each of them, the relationship was built on mutual care and mutual concern, on mutual responsibility and respect for independence, both theirs and mine. It was a good model for human relationships, as well.

We became a part of each other's lives. And that reality made the world better, the country more moral, if only by one small relationship at a time.

I know that because of each of my animal companions my

own small soul has been awakened to more of life than I could have ever found without them. The thought of using them, or any like them, with no regard for their pain, their needs, their strengths, their devotion, has become increasingly impossible over the years.

Clearly, Gandhi was right: "The greatness of a nation and its moral progress can be judged by the way its animals are treated."

I am convinced, thanks to Danny, Duffy, and Lady, that we can all be better people when we finally include the rights of animals in our own criteria for greatness.

If we will only learn to see beyond our own world and into theirs.

A PRAYER FOR ANIMALS

Joan Chittister

Great God,
you have gifted us with a presence
in our lives
to save us from ourselves.

You have given us animals
whose lives speak to us
of devotion and heart
of patient endurance
of the power of faithful presence and
of love without reason.

Give us, great and gentle God,
the caring appreciation
of those creatures
who model for us
your companionship and protection
as well as your personal care.

We have seen in them, loving God,
the stability of commitment
and the greatness of trust
that we owe you.

For the joy they have brought us
and the faith in humanity
they have shown us
we thank you, our God.

In them we sense
the goodness of the cosmos

the graciousness of your creation
and insight into the sacredness
of our own animal nature.

For that we are forever grateful.

Tempted to take
the creatures of the world for granted
inclined to treat them more as property
than present signs
of your life and love
give us the grace, O God,
to forever care for them
as you have cared for us.

We see in them living signs
of the network of nature
of which we are only a part.

May you, great God who made them,
reward them
with good caretakers
with bright sun and days of play
with a comfortable old age
with the love they deserve
for having so faithfully loved us.

Give us the vision
to squander our love on others
as they have squandered theirs on us.

For all of them, great God,
we give you thanks
and see the glory
of you glowing in them, as well.

Amen.

ACKNOWLEDGEMENTS

There are some books that write themselves. They are so obvious, so universally true, and at the same time so personal that they simply flow out onto the page, open and honest and easy. This is one of them. It is, I have come to realize, the story of a journey through life with animal friends as well as professional colleagues and personal acquaintances for companions. It's about a part of life that is wordless, this bond between humans and animals, but not without meaning; often unrecognized socially, it is, nevertheless, not without deep affection. It is spoken about rarely, perhaps, but not because there is no genuine attachment between us.

On the contrary, this book explores the deeper relationship that comes from getting to know an animal friend and allowing that friend to know you, too. It calls us to assess our attitudes toward animals. Most of all, it calls us to recognize what they have been teaching us subconsciously, perhaps, but always clearly as we go through life together.

It is a call to explore the spiritual impact of this human-animal relationship on us all: its lessons, its meanings and its challenges.

As with every other manuscript I produce, I spend a lot of time with selected readers before publication. For this particular book, I chose readers both because they liked animals and because they didn't; because they had lived with animals themselves or because they couldn't even imagine agreeing to do so.

From each of those different perspectives I came away satisfied that we all have something to learn and to share from assessing the way we see animals—or do not see them at all. Each of these readers added a dimension of experience and insight that gave depth to a topic that is also funny, sad, enlightening, and spiritual to the core. Those distinct perspectives will surely affect the way all of us deal with the land, its life forms, and the very future of the planet, as well.

And so, I thank all these readers in a special way for taking time with this manuscript to make it richer of spirit and more meaningful to us all.

They include: Fred Burnham, Jo Clarke, Judith Davis, Paul Ferris, Hank Kriegel, Kathy Schatzberg, Susan Smith and Mary Hembrow Snyder.

In a special way I want to thank Elizabeth and William Vorsheck, and Gail Freyne for the physical support and encouragement that have made this book, and so much else in my life, possible, as well.

I want to mention in particular the sisters who bring this work to its final form: Maureen Tobin, OSB, Mary Lou Kownacki, OSB and Susan Doubet, OSB. It's their kind of commitment that makes my own work possible.

And I thank the readers of this work, too, who in it may begin to see their own extended families of children, adults, and animals as the real teachers of the wholeness of life. Otherwise, the fact that we are fast becoming separated from life in its best and broadest forms may escape us all.

Our awareness of what it really means to be alive is being smothered by the antiseptic and the mechanical, by the virtual and the robotic. We have come to live lives far too technological, far too isolated from the land. We have become far too rational to recognize the gifts that come from the affection, humor, spirit, and instincts of the animal friends with whom we share the planet.

May we become sensitive to otherness. May we become open to new kinds of wonder. May we learn to appreciate gifts not our own. Then, fully aware of our animal companions who have learned to inhabit our world a great deal better than we have learned to respect theirs, we ourselves will grow in stature.

May we all discover how to stretch ourselves beyond the boundaries of the human in order to become more human, more humane, than ever before.